Wanderful

Wanderful

THE MODERN BOHEMIAN'S GUIDE TO TRAVELING IN STYLE

ANDI EATON

ABRAMS IMAGE | NEW YORK

Editor: Cristina Garces
Designer: Jenny Kraemer
Production Manager: Kathleen
Gaffney

Library of Congress Control Number:
2017930315

ISBN: 978-1-4197-2676-7

Printed and bound in China
10 9 8 7 6 5 4 3 2 1

Abrams Image books are available at
special discounts when purchased in
quantity for premiums and promotions
as well as fundraising or educational
use. Special editions can also be
created to specification. For details,
contact specialsales@abramsbooks.
com or the address below.

ABRAMS
The Art of Books

115 West 18th Street
New York, NY 10011
abramsbooks.com

TABLE OF CONTENTS

THE ROUTES

intro

I SOMETIMES ENVY the way things were for travelers of earlier generations—a time before the Internet when interesting destinations were found in dog-eared guides and by word of mouth. At some point, amid the rise of the Internet travel guide and the invention of Yelp and Google, travel, especially by car, lost that sense of exploration and discovery.

WHEN YOU'RE TRAVELING, YOU ARE WHAT YOU ARE RIGHT THERE AND THEN. —WILLIAM LEAST HEAT-MOON

Growing up as the oldest child born into a family of travelers, I never felt settled—I expected, as soon as I was old enough, to find a road map to the stars and take off, skipping around the world. My grandparents on both sides always had those travel maps stretched across the walls. Full of colorful pins, each told stories of destinations known and unknown.

At the age of seven, I discovered my own "travel maps" of sorts in the pages of the magazines I found at the bottom of my mother's wardrobe one afternoon. Those pages transported me to dream worlds that I wanted so much to be a part of my everyday life. The late afternoon perusals that followed jump-started a style obsession that has become a lifelong study. Many years and a couple hundred pounds of *Vogue* later, my studio is an explosion of color, fabrics, and editorial photo ideas. The images I return to over and over represent a global style, one that is influenced by different cultures and an array of destinations. As a wayfaring girl with a love of fashion, travel has become my vehicle for style exploration.

Have you ever played that childhood game where you spin the globe, eyes closed, and decide that wherever it stops will be your future destination? Once I was old enough to choose my own destiny, I decided to make that game my reality—to turn my wanderlust into an opportunity to explore my deep adoration of style and the world at large. I wanted to live like a modern bohemian with a mindset of artistic survival: always on the hunt for the next destination for inspiration, the next tour, the next show.

I have always looked to bohemians, flower children, and artists for travel and style inspiration: What are their favorite lunch-counter dives and vintage shops? Where are the musicians late-night dancing after the last encore? And most importantly, what are they wearing while they do it?

A few years ago, I took off to spend the summer traveling. To prepare, I did research using standard travel books, magazines, and lots of Google searching for travel blog posts on my intended destinations. I tried the usual suspects, of course— *Lonely Planet, Frommer's, Condé Nast Traveler*—and there is certainly a reason for the success of these publications. People want the tips, and they want the lists of the best restaurants and bars, museums to visit, and tours to take. However, I wanted to

spin the globe and
chase the stars!

experience a deeper, more authentic connection to each locale than what I was finding in the guides available to me. So, I decided to write my own.

This book is meant to be the BFF's guide to the best, and most fashionable, American road trips ever. Throughout nine routes in locales by the sea, in the desert, and in the forest, this fashion travelogue will make you feel like you're traipsing across the country with your best, and best-dressed, girlfriends by your side. We'll be traveling to America's most stylish, unique, and hidden destinations together, and I, along with fellow fashion mavens, artists, bohemians, and wanderers, will share photos and stories to guide you to the best, shopping, dining, music, and fun, just like a local. Each section has mountains and valleys and long winding roads. There are small towns and big cities, too. No matter your inclination, there's a fashion-filled trip for you!

The routes in this book are designed for three types of travelers:

THE FREE-SPIRITED WANDERER: This adventure is for the road trip warrior who plans to spend a week or more on the road. Each trip, followed verbatim, is designed for this type of traveler. The wanderer packs up the RV or the SUV and takes the scenic route to every destination. She wears velvet in the summertime and glitter on her eyes, and she loves nostalgia and the stories of the beatniks and Gertrude Stein.

THE (LONG) WEEKEND TRAVELER: If you're planning for travels that will last only a few days, choose a few of the features in each route for a three- to four-day adventure. The weekender girl hops a plane to follow her favorite band or takes off for a few days of junk-shop thrifting. She has an intense love of style and culture. For the long weekend edit of each trip, choose the art galleries, coffee shops, and late-night hangs in the up-and-coming neighborhoods.

THE DAY(S) TRIPPER: Each route includes destinations perfect for one- to two-day trips full of must-see points of interest, as well as local favorites. This journey is perfect for the girl heading out on a whim for a day or two with friends, a girl who's ready to throw her bathing suit and a dip-dyed caftan in the car and take off. She loves spontaneous trips to the coast and jaunts to the big cities. She's forever game for an adventure on a budget.

A note: For the most part, the iconic tourist destinations aren't included on our routes. Yes, we're going to the Grand Canyon and the French Quarter of New Orleans, but we're also hitting the artistic desert hideaways and roadside dance halls. The mission here is to travel slow with good friends and to make time for a mystical experience. That said, if you've got "bucket list" places to visit that fall along these routes, of course, go!

So pack a cute bag, throw on your flowiest dress, and get ready to hit the road for a stylish adventure!

THE
WANDERFUL
GIRL

The "Wanderful Girl" is a modern bohemian. She's a nomadic bon vivant collecting perspective and style inspiration from around the globe. The wanderful girl has the spirit of an old west explorer and the eye of a budding artist. She is a lover of mountains, seas, cities, and all the in-betweens. She makes her home in the grand bazaar of the world, finding magic in the mundane. She's the girl dancing around a campfire in a vintage gown, having her palm read while sipping wine from a plastic cup. She brings her record player on her road trips and knows every Stevie Nicks song by heart. She's delicately nostalgic and playfully potent; she lives every day with wild abandon.

creating

YOUR OWN
WANDERFUL LIFE

TO GET STARTED on a path to living your most fashionable and adventurous life, here are some basic philosophies that are worth embracing, whether you're a modern nomad or an armchair traveler with a bohemian heart.

FIND BEAUTY IN IMPERFECTION: Study *wabi-sabi*—a Japanese worldview centered on seeing the beauty in imperfection and accepting the natural cycle of life. This philosophy will inspire you to find joy in collecting quirky souvenirs like flea market tea towels and wilted flowers pressed between pages of an old book. It will remind you to embrace the moments when things go wrong as part of the traveling experience.

ONE DAY
WE WILL
TALK ABOUT
HOW OUR
BLUE MOON
WISH CAME
TRUE. HOW
WHEN THE
UNIVERSE
FINALLY
RELEASED
THE PINS
THAT HELD
US SO
REMOTE,
WE DID NOT
FALL SUD-
DENLY & ALL
AT ONCE,
BUT RATHER
DRIFTED
TOWARDS
EACH OTHER
WITH THE
WHIMSICAL
GRACE OF
DANDELION
CLOCKS.
—AMANDA
TORRONI

BE PRESENT: Focus fully on the moment; people and places bloom when bestowed with heartfelt attention. Connect deliberately to nature and everyone in it, remembering that every person and thing came from somewhere.

FOCUS ON THE POSSIBILITIES: Every moment is an opportunity to experience something new. Take life's little surprises in stride, especially when things don't go your way. Remember that good or bad, everything is temporary—it's all about how we spin it to ourselves.

FIND HAPPINESS IN CURIOSITY: Choose a path of constant learning and allow new experiences to shape you. Open up to astrology, astronomy, and philosophy, and learn to live without the habitual draw of technological consumption.

TRAVEL LIGHT: Figuratively and literally, be free of the things that weigh you down. Give up the unnecessary material possessions and foster relationships that are passionate and invite growth. Liberate with love the things that hold you back.

Now that you're in the right headspace, it's time to start packing so we can get our journey under way.

packing

LIKE A ROCK STAR

H O W   D O the artists, musicians, and style mavens who spend so much of their time living out of a suitcase decide what to pack? What's in their daily regime that keeps their skin glowing, and how do they achieve such effortlessly chic style? We've all seen the photos, and there's so much to be said for looking fresh, natural, and a bit undone. These traveling fashion-istas so often have a signature—a color, a scent, the way they tie their hair back, or some discreet little accessory. They know what style elements work for them, and they own it.

These girls give us immediate lifestyle envy when we see their travel photos. Want to live inside those Instagrams? Here's a peek inside the bags of stylish wanderers—dive in to get inspiration for packing, dressing, and hanging like them!

As I began planning for the routes I cover in this book, I really did my research: I wanted to study modern bohemians in their natural habitats in order to figure out the kind of things real girls need to achieve perfect travel style. So I made a few of my wanderful friends the subjects of an in-depth anthropological study. I excavated the beauty products at the bottoms of their makeup bags. I deconstructed their closets to analyze their aesthetic. I watched them pack up art supplies, photo equipment, and musical instruments. And in the end, I discovered the essentials for a perfect adventure on the road.

TRAVEL PARTNERS

Throughout the road trips in this book, I split my time among three traveling partners:

◀ ALLISTER ANN: A photographer and director by day, an ethereal wildflower of a girl by night.

▼ BEN ALLEMAN: A tour-bus-living musician with an electric cowboy style. A mariachi jacket layered over tie-dye? It's his grocery store attire.

▸KEIKO LYNN:
A makeup maven and indie fashionista with the swoon-worthiest closet on planet Earth.

They taught me that the first thing on the "Essentials" list is to find your travel soulmate, a person who can turn an ordinary trip into a magical odyssey. Once you've got them, you're ready to get packing.

THE BAGS

Bags are the first items to cross off your list. For wanderers on lengthier trips, you'll need your largest duffel bag, a weekender, and a backpack. This combination will allow you to maximize trunk space and will tuck easily around the rest of your gear. You'll want the extra room for the fun stuff: picnic baskets, piles of patchwork, and billowy blankets (you'll need extras to build beach teepees), plus your vinyl collection and portable player.

THE DUFFEL

Herschel Supply Company, Pendleton, Elliott Lucca, and Coach make great duffels that are perfect for just about a week's worth of traveling essentials.

THE WEEKENDER

This bag is classic, easy to pack on a whim, and the perfect size for any adventure. Hobo the Original, Everlane, Cuyana, and Sóle Society all have great options.

THE BACKPACK

The backpack serves as a place for the everyday things you'll need while you explore each location.

polaroid camera
favorite book
headphones
motel key
rose-flavored lip gloss
vintage hair pins
extra cash
postcards for friends

THE CLOTHES

No matter your style at home—glamour girl, classics lover, minimalist, sporty chic—when you're on the road, allow your mood, whims, fantasies, and destination to drive what you wear.

The best travel style isn't overdone—basic T-shirts, denim, breathable maxi dresses, and lots of layers are truly all you'll need. For a week on the road, pack two pairs of black leggings, three to four classic T-shirts, your favorite sunglasses and a backup pair, and items from the categories to follow. Once you've laid everything out, take a few moments to edit—it's the everyday versatile things that you'll be glad you have along.

T-SHIRTS & TOPS

Used as a quintessential layering piece or worn on its own, a neutral cotton T-shirt or blouse can be worn every single day in a variety of ways. Dress it down with a pair of cutoffs or up with a maxi skirt. Add a scarf or a pile of kitschy brooches and

DAD WOULD MIX A MEXICAN TUNIC AND BIRKENSTOCKS WITH CHIC, CENTER-PLEATED KHAKI PANTS AND A GOLD ROLEX.
—AMANDA BROOKS

krystal, a friend and
wanderful muse, has the
dreamiest travel wardrobe

pins to create multiple outfits from the same top. You can't ever have enough of the basic variety; however, collectible T-shirts (think band or vintage) will give your outfits a special, personal touch.

DENIM

The ultimate classic: Invest in quality designer denim and vintage denim classics. Light wash, dark wash, denim jackets, overalls, and everything in between—denim is always in style.

SHORTS

Layer over tights or leggings in cooler climates. The same pair of cutoffs can transition from your beach wear to your after-hours look with a quick accessory change.

DRESSES

A basic tip is to stick to little black dresses in a few style varieties. But here's where traveling fashionistas can step way out of the norm: Dresses take up so little space, which makes it easy to pack several. Make heads turn by choosing dresses designed in vintage styles that make a statement: prints and patterns inspired by flora and fauna found along your travel route are beautiful options.

MY PACKING LIST: FIRST AND FOREMOST, AN EPIC PLAYLIST. THEN, HIKING GEAR TO THROW ON IN A MOMENT'S NOTICE— ALWAYS BE PREPARED TO HEAD OUT AND PLAY!
—KRYSTAL BICK, THIS TIME TOMORROW

floral mini—perfect for twirling!

COATS & JACKETS

Check the weather and know the conditions before you go. During every season but winter, you can likely get by with a lightweight jacket and something a bit heavier to throw on top for cooler days—this will lessen the load in your bag.

FOOTWEAR

In the travel bags of the style gurus you'll meet on our routes, I found a common shoe theme: Every fashionista carried pairs of ankle boots, ballet flats, leather sandals, and classic sneakers. In one case, I found that only one pair of shoes made the cut: meticulously hand-crafted vintage Lucchese boots. As this particular fashion maven musician twirled onto stage as her set began, it was clear that to her, that pair of boots was all she'd ever need. A good general rule is to pack one pair of boots, one pair of sandals, and something a little more posh for all-night dance parties.

ACCESSORIES

JEWELRY: Leave expensive or sentimental pieces at home for safekeeping. Instead, include a few statement pieces in your bag—cocktail rings or dainty stackables are good choices—and then pair those with basic studs or hoops. A favorite activity of mine is to find special items on my travels, like local turquoise or hand-carved beads, and wear those along the way.

SCARVES: If you'll be spending a lot of time outside or are planning to go to a theater or venue with a pumping A/C system, it'll be totally worth packing several of these. Oversize scarves will also double as blankets or towels.

HATS: Hats are such a statement-making signature accessory. The right hat can reinvent an outfit while also salvaging second-day hair, too.

SUNGLASSES: The most stylish fashionistas wear sunglasses of all styles and sizes. Think about practicality when packing a pair or two, and keep in mind that the perfect sunnies are versatile and will tie your full look together.

BEAUTY ESSENTIALS

Be sure to pack your usual basics and a few signature items, too (a vibrant lip color for example). For a well-stocked bag, pack a few of these bonus items:

SURVIVAL ESSENTIALS

The routes in this book will take you to all different terrains across the country. Here are a few suggestions to make sure you're never stranded without essentials:

- ☐ essential oils (lavender, patchouli, and eucalyptus are favorites)
- ☐ spf (protect your skin!)
- ☐ all-in-one creams or mists
- ☐ dr. bronners magic soap (works on everything!)
- ☐ tiger balm (soothing after long hikes)

- ☐ phone map apps
- ☐ paper maps
- ☐ energy-packed snacks
- ☐ jumper cables
- ☐ tire patch kit
- ☐ flashlight
- ☐ batteries
- ☐ lots of h2o!

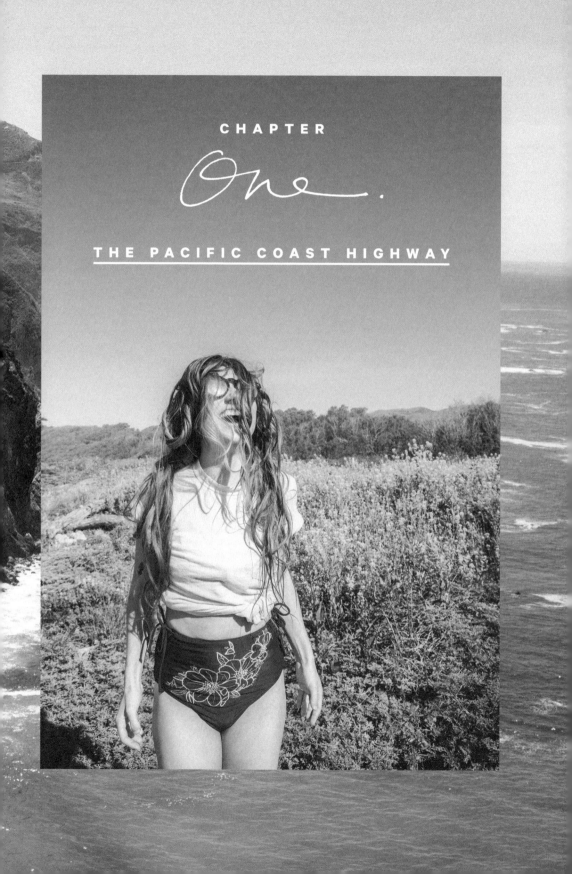

CHAPTER

One.

THE PACIFIC COAST HIGHWAY

THE WONDROUS THING about the West Coast is how you can spend hours driving along the Pacific Coast Highway—the open and free roads tucked in between San Francisco and Los Angeles, two of California's most energetic and wildly different cities. This deliriously beautiful route includes popular locales as well as the farmlands and roadside towns in between. Along the way, we'll experience the electromagnetic forces of Ojai, work as a farmhand at a valley ranch, enjoy the kitschy opulence of the Madonna Inn, and twist along Highway 1 through the rocky cliffs and giant redwoods with Big Sur's modern-day artists and musicians.

the enchanting overlook. stay for the sunset!

THE CALIFORNIA FLOWER CHILD

THE CALIFORNIA GIRL loves palm trees and giant redwoods, beach boys and mountain men. She's as comfortable in vintage roller skates as she is setting up for a night of roadside glamping. She hears music in the waves and takes inspiration from all that she encounters, from the boardwalks to the surf breaks. Her style is boho-chic youth: skateboarder by day, moon-dancing flower child by night.

SHE IS FREE IN HER WILDNESS, SHE IS A WANDERESS, A DROP OF FREE WATER. —ROMAN PAYNE

the California flower child
CAPSULE WARDROBE

For seaside adventures

Floral-print flare dresses

Festive shorts sets

Hemp T-shirts

Wide-leg pants with a paper-bag waist

High-waisted bikinis

For valley days

Long-sleeve flannel shirts paired with skinny jeans

Gauzy maxi dresses layered with unexpected outerwear

Denim midi skirts and lace-trimmed crop tops

Shoulder-baring lace dresses for vineyard evenings

Footwear and accessories

Cowboy boots

Skater sneakers

Gold gladiator sandals

Birkenstocks

Mix-and-match stackable rings

Delicate cuffs and studs

Ribbon and vintage belts

Worn-in baseball caps

For beach-to-street layering

Ornately decorated capes

Velvet jackets with elaborate appliqués

the California
flower child
LOVES...

PCH VIBES
PLAYLIST:

▶ "California
Dreamin'"
(The Mamas &
The Papas)

▶ "Ojai" (Ray
LaMontagne)

▶ "Forget You
in LA" (Poema)

▶ "Hotel
California"
(Eagles)

▶ "Going to
California"
(Led Zeppelin)

▶ "California"
(Phantom
Planet)

▶ "San
Francisco"
(Scott
McKenzie)

▶ "Carry On"
(Bjorn and
the Sun)

▶ "California"
(Joni Mitchell)

▶ "California
Girls" (The
Beach Boys)

MOVIES: *Somewhere* (2010), *Vertigo* (1958), *Clueless* (1995), *Gidget* (1959), *Fast Times at Ridgemont High* (1982), *American Graffiti* (1973), *Valley Girl* (1983), *The Long Goodbye* (1973), *Sideways* (2004), *Valley of the Dolls* (1967)

READS: *Big Sur and the Oranges of Hieronymus Bosch* (Henry Miller), *Where I Was From* (Joan Didion), *Tortilla Flat* (John Steinbeck), *Big Sur* (Jack Kerouac), *The Selected Poetry of Robinson Jeffers,* the *Sweet Valley High* series

BANDS: Haim, The Byrds, The Beach Boys, Sublime, Red Hot Chili Peppers, Black Rebel Motorcycle Club, Rilo Kiley, The Bangles, Best Coast

THE ROUTE

THE FREE-SPIRITED WANDERER: Highway 1 runs along most of the California coast up to Washington. For our trip, we'll be traveling the Pacific Coast Highway portion. We're flying into Los Angeles and then heading north on California 101 toward Ojai Valley. Leaving Ojai, travel north to San Luis Obispo, along Highway 1 to Big Sur, and finally end in San Francisco. Each stop is a two- to three-hour drive depending on how often you stop to take in the view and how many RVs are cruising ahead of you.

THE LONG WEEKENDER: Choose two destinations and plan on spending two days or so in each! Traveling by car, start in LA and head north to either Ojai or San Luis Obispo. Or, start in San Francisco and drive south to Big Sur.

THE DAY(S) TRIPPER: Choose one destination and plan on spending all of your time there. Flights to San Francisco are abundant from most parts of the country. Several municipal airports along the route (Monterey County, SLO) are closer options for Big Sur and San Luis Obispo.

OJAI VALLEY, CA

The Chumash natives named the valley for the moon (*'awhaÿ*), which rises high at night, creating a famous pink glow. Ojai is a mecca for earthy artists and fashion mavens; let's be honest, anyone who follows the fashion-forward Instagrammers of LA knows of its natural beauty—it's where Angelenos come to shake off the madness of urban life. It's a paradisiacal destination for a weekend of porch-style concerts, horseback riding, spa days, tangerines (the groves are everywhere), and hiking the backcountry. Much of Ojai's famous quietude comes from its location at the southern end of Los Padres National Forest,

which extends uninterrupted for some two hundred miles north, from the Topatopa Mountains to the cliffs of Big Sur.

Chain stores (other than a few gas stations and banks) are prohibited by law, and the galleries and boutique shops featuring locally made wares are luxurious and abundant. The vibe is old-school bohemian California blended with modern-day urban farmer, and the little downtown corridor's hoi polloi are handsome rancher types (with tattoos and cowboy boots) and gorgeous art girls on solace-searching retreats.

Jeep

WHAT TO WEAR
IN OJAI

The Ojai girl's style? Elevated hippie, living on fresh juices and homemade beauty products made with coconut and avocado oils. The Ojai girl loves the ethereal feel of a maxi skirt paired with a gladiator sandal and a simple silk tank. She knows how to extend her summer wardrobe well into the barely cooler days of fall and winter with subtle layers. She'll pair denim and a white button down over a classic one-piece bathing suit, always prepared for an afternoon in the waterfalls and swimming holes of Matilija Canyon.

A DAY IN OJAI

HIP VEGAN: This cute café is perfect for a midmorning pick-me-up: Order Vietnamese iced coffee made with coconut milk paired with divine tangerine-marmalade cookie bars. When you're done, dig through the adorable vintage/thrift shop next door.

BART'S BOOKS: Schedule a solid hour to explore this open-air bookstore that's been operating in the same location since the 1960s. It's the largest independently operated outdoor bookstore in the country, its inception a result of Richard "Bart" Bartinsdale's overgrown collection of books making their way out onto his sidewalk. Bart's Books now boasts an inventory of nearly one million books, ranging from the thirty-five-cent specials that line the outside walls to rare, out-of-print first editions valued in the thousands of dollars.

BOCCALI'S: Serving up Italian family dishes, Boccali's is nestled between two peaks overlooking the valley beneath the shade of hundred-year-old oaks. Positioned on a mountainside curve, the restaurant has a garden out back that provides fresh produce for their homemade pizza and pasta, perfect for a late lunch.

SUNSET ON SISAR CREEK: End the day with a hike along upper Sisar Creek, which has magnificent tree canopies and little streams for an evening picnic. Direct your gaze east toward the bluffs of the Topatopa Mountains to catch the sun's reflection at dusk, a time locals refer to as "pink moments."

OJAI RANCHO INN: Right off the main drag, the Ojai Rancho Inn has a chic little lobby that doubles as a mini boutique. Check in to this charming place for the evening, where cactus plants line the fireplace and palo santo is for sale at the check-in desk. The vibe is distinctly rustic (but the rooms still have Jacuzzi tubs).

refresh your mind at heart's

CAN'T-MISS OJAI

FOR THE FASHIONISTA: Make time for a visit to Shop Summer Camp, a former gas station converted into a little lifestyle and frame shop that features a perfect Americana mix of jewelry, art, vintage clothing, and home décor. Pick up a handmade keychain or a candle as an Ojai souvenir.

FOR THE SPIRITUALIST: Spend a few hours on Meditation Mount—thirty-two acres of sacred, open-to-the-public meditation space that's been around since the 1970s. Take in the view at Vista Point and sneak into one of the tangerine farms to walk along the groves.

FOR THE ART AFICIONADO: As an artists' retreat, Ojai is remarkably different from other art destinations. It doesn't feel like a tourist stop, and there's a warm synergy between the spirit seekers, the makers, and the ranchers living off the land. Stroll around the village galleries and spend a few hours in the Ojai Valley Museum to become one with the thriving arts community and world-renowned artists who make their home here.

In the morning, load the car with your tangerine marmalade and your stack of photography books and vintage maps from

Bart's, throw a few flowers gathered from the roadside on the dashboard, and head north to San Luis Obispo.

101 N from Ojai to San Luis Obispo area (approx. 70 miles, 1 hour)

SAN LUIS OBISPO, CA

Traveling to San Luis Obispo, the rolling green hills are as awe-inspiring as the views of the cerulean Pacific. It's home to many beautiful beaches (Pismo Beach or Morro Bay) and wine country vineyards (Paso Robles is a favorite).

AN AFTERNOON IN SAN LUIS OBISPO

POINT SAN LUIS LIGHTHOUSE: This thirty-acre nature preserve is a secret gem on the Central Coast on the harbor near Avila Beach. Take the trolley ride in to visit the beautifully restored lighthouse and the surrounding coastal area.

WINE TASTING: There is an abundance of dazzling wineries in the area, sure to satisfy any pace and taste. San Luis Obispo is known for its sparkling varieties of wine. There are eight or so vineyards in the San Luis Obispo Sparkling Wine Guide and six other wine trails that wind through the city and surrounding areas. Paso Robles wine country, just a little way outside of San Luis Obispo, is home to more than two hundred wineries, mostly comprising boutique and small family-owned vineyards.

FREMONT THEATRE: Catch a show at the Art Deco historic theater that looks like something out of a Sofia Coppola film. The opulent theater hosts classic films, up-and-coming indie musicians, and throwback rock bands on a nightly rotation.

HEARST CASTLE: Originally built as the private estate of media mogul William Randolph Hearst, the castle is now a state park with decadently lavish furnishings, a grand art collection, and more than one hundred acres of gardens. Exotic creatures roam the property, which once housed the world's largest private zoo.

Point San Luis Lighthouse

541.788.1497   jesse@sanluisl

www.sanluislighth

wine!

VINA ROBL

VACANCY

COCKTAILS

COPPER
CAFE
Pastries
STEAK
Hot

Madonna Inn
100 MADONNA ROAD • SAN LUIS OBISPO • CALIFORNIA 93401

coffee ✓

pink champagne
cake ✓

extra pastries
for the road ✓

MADONNA INN: Make a reservation at the Madonna Inn, an extravagant motel unlike anything else in the country. Alex and Phyllis Madonna opened the flamboyantly pink Madonna Inn in 1958. Originally twelve rooms, the most over-the-top motel you'll ever step foot in was built to its current specs after a fire burned the original place down in 1966. The amenities here include a heated pool and hot tubs, a day spa, a wine cellar, and a bakery offering pink champagne cake and the most delicious morning pastries (get there early for the best selection!).

Each of the 110 rooms is themed as if lifted straight from the pages of a quirky cult Western, and the lodgers are notorious characters in their own right. With so many options, which to choose? If you're staying more than a night, switch rooms each night—and yes, the inn practically encourages it!

Alex was a ranching partner to actor John Wayne, and the "Pick & Shovel" is the official cattle brand for the inn. The suite of the same name is one of the inn's most popular suites, located just above the horse pastures. It features wall-to-wall leather couches and bunk beds for sleepover guests. A cowboy we encountered on our way to the dance hall told us that he had been coming to the Madonna Inn since the 1960s just to host parties in this suite.

Other favorites include the Canary Room, adorned with vibrant yellow canary cage light fixtures and velvet floral prints, the Barrel of Fun, featuring sequin-textured walls, and the Starlite, a room awash in silvery blues with its own fourth-floor entrance up a white spiral staircase.

101 N from San Luis Obispo to Camatta Ranch (approx. 35 miles)

ANYBODY CAN BUILD ONE ROOM AND A THOUSAND LIKE IT. I WANT PEOPLE TO COME IN WITH A SMILE AND LEAVE WITH A SMILE. IT'S FUN. WHAT FUN DO YOU THINK PAUL GETTY GOT OUT OF HIS LIFE?
—ALEX MADONNA

CAMATTA RANCH, CA

The family farm of Felicia and Mark Morrison, just a short ride into the valley from San Luis Obispo, dates back to the 1846 Mexican land grant days. The Morrisons purchased the fifty-square-mile ranch (which is larger than San Francisco, by the way) in 1978, and it's presently available to rent, Airbnb-style, for farm stays, concerts, shows, and parties.

While there, stay in the Buffalo Bungalow, a watering hole that the buffalo herd visits each evening, hike Fossil Hill, a trail that is home to million-year-old sea fossils, or venture out on the safari truck to meet Mark's extensive collection of gypsy wagons, ancient cabins, and vintage cars.

On our visit, we met the Morrison's daughter, Emilee, an earthy bohemian poster child. We spent a day as farmhands to Emilee, bottle-feeding a baby deer brought in for rehabilitation and tending to the thirty-two acres of exotic and native animals. Upon departure, pack extra slices of Felicia's homemade blueberry bread into your picnic basket, and begin your trek north to the wildness of Big Sur.

1 N from Camatta Ranch to Big Sur (approx. 125 miles, 3 hours)

emilee caring for the babes. sweet stormy, a corsican mouflon, is the star of the barn

BIG SUR, CA

Big Sur's magnitude is supernatural. The ninety-mile renegade coastline is soaked in a perpetual summer fog, dipping directly below ancient trees that are the tallest on earth. Traveling up Highway 1, you're immediately transported back to the bohemian artist's off-the-grid Big Sur.

Plan for a spring visit, when the wildflowers are in bloom (so beautiful, they will literally make you pull your car over) and the tourist RVs aren't quite taking over the roads yet. Plan ahead and reserve a camp site, and you'll be practicing your glamping skills in one of the most wonderfully mind-boggling places you'll ever experience.

When planning your trip, keep in mind that your iPhone is only good for taking photos or storing screenshots of campsites and directions. You'll need a physical map, day-hike supplies, some books, and an Internet-free form of music if you plan to spend a day out on the beach or in the woods. Here, cell-phone service disappears. It's not a spotty signal—there's absolutely no service for miles and hours. Before making the drive, which will include the most panoramic views of coastal cliffs, be sure to stop for gas and supplies. There are no town squares, no traffic lights, certainly no strip malls, and you can't exactly pinpoint Big Sur on a map.

WHAT TO WEAR IN BIG SUR

During the day, the Big Sur girl is always in her bathing suit, with cutoffs and an assortment of breathable layers and hemp cotton T-shirts thrown on top. She wraps her hair in a tribal-inspired oversize scarf and wears handmade friendship bracelets she's collected for years. At night, she channels storybook forest fairies and glows in ethereal dresses trimmed in romantic macramé-lace.

If you're used to the normal pace of the technologically connected life, as most of us are, you may experience a little panic. However, Big Sur residents are known for being gracious hosts. They get excited about everything—a skunk wanders through the forest high on some sort of poisonous mushroom, and it's the talk of the coffee shop for the day. It's a magical place.

So how do you best guide your experience in a place that's so untouched, that's as much of a state of mind as it is a location? Commit to respecting the land, the forest, the untamed ocean, and every single rock as if it were your own. After all, it is really. It's all ours.

surf's up! ♡

not a soul on the beach,
except us and a surfer
still sleeping off
last night's swells

TWO DAYS IN BIG SUR

GLEN OAKS: Stay in one of these Big Sur cabins nestled under tall redwood trees on a wooded lane across from the river. From the eco-friendly custom-designed living room, you'll have views of a lush grove encircled by redwood trees. Make s'mores in your private wood-stocked fire pit and soak at night in the outdoor clawfoot tubs. Glen Oaks offers glamping options on their property, too.

BIG SUR ROADHOUSE: Visit to lounge with the local set. You can also grab lunch, coffee, and wine from the seasonal menu. We met songstress and Reiki healer Kristen Gradwohl here for a perfect day of what she called "intuitive floating."

FERNWOOD RESORT: Stop by for a bite at the tavern and live music in the evenings. The general store and espresso bar here will also help you get fully stocked for each day.

NEPENTHE: Nepenthe sits a thousand feet or so above the Pacific. Named for the mythical drug that causes one to forget all sorrows, the restaurant and bar is built on huge boulders with walls of plate glass, like something out of a 1950s spy movie.

CAN'T-MISS BIG SUR

FOR THE SPIRITUALIST: Stop by Esalen Institute, home to the Big Sur Folk Festival of 1969. Visit the hot springs during public hours or book an Esalen program for the full experience.

FOR THE BIBLIOPHILE: Head to the Henry Miller Memorial Library to explore the quirky collection of artifacts, memorabilia, and books by and about the author. Read Miller's autobiographical notes lining the walls of the interior. The library serves as a public gallery, performance, and workshop space—a place to mingle with the resident locals (and cat) while sipping complimentary coffee.

FOR THE NATURALIST: Hike at one of Big Sur's California State Parks: Limekiln, Julia Pfeiffer Burns, or Andrew Molera. For a spectacular view, head to Pfeiffer Big Sur State Park and take the two-mile Pfeiffer Falls trail ending at a sixty-foot waterfall. Then, continue up to Valley View trail for look-out points. For the beach lover, head to Andrew Molera for the Rivermouth surf spot, camping, and a secluded beach.

ON SOFT SPRING NIGHTS I'LL STAND IN THE YARD UNDER THE STARS— SOMETHING GOOD WILL COME OUT OF ALL THINGS YET—AND IT WILL BE GOLDEN AND ETER-NAL JUST LIKE THAT— THERE'S NO NEED TO SAY ANOTHER WORD.
—JACK KEROUAC

FOR THE COMMUNITY SEEKER: The Big Sur Grange hosts First Saturday Pop-Up Bakeries, the Harvest Craft Fair, and local theater and benefit shows. Founded in 1948, its mission is to promote the economic and political well-being of farming communities.

FOR THE SWEETS CONNOISSEUR: Big Sur Bakery serves up fresh bread and pastries, a strong cup of coffee, homemade granola, herb-filled omelets, and a full rustic-style menu all day long.

End your visit with a leisurely drive up the Pacific Coast Highway past the Pigeon Point lighthouse all the way to San Francisco. Make time to stop to take in one last view of the mountainsides and bridges sitting high above the barrel-shaped waves crashing below.

1 N from Big Sur to San Francisco (approx. 140 miles, 3.5 hours)

kristen plays a song under the old redwood trees

SAN FRANCISCO, CA

San Francisco is a charismatic rarity. There is a vitality, a love, and even a moodiness that permeates the city. Flashback to the Summer of Love: 1967, a cultural revolution, young people from all across America pouring into the Haight-Ashbury neighborhood and creating a new way of living, a free society. The hippie counter-culture began in San Francisco, and that feeling of freedom still spills today from the people, the architecture, the food and drinks, and most certainly the music and fashion. San Francisco is a mecca of cool, and it's that way without even trying.

There are so many amazing neighborhoods in San Francisco, but with twenty-four hours to experience the city, we'll start in the popular Mission District and then venture out to a few other more obscure neighborhoods. The beauty of a San Francisco visit is that even in a day, no matter which neighborhood or neighborhoods you choose, it's a dreamer's playground of a place to spend a little time.

SAN FRANCISCO ITSELF IS ART.... EVERY BLOCK IS A SHORT STORY, EVERY HILL A NOVEL. EVERY HOME A POEM, EVERY DWELLER WITHIN IMMORTAL.
—WILLIAM SAROYAN

SAN FRANCISCO IN A DAY

TARTINE: Start the day with the legendary and absolutely heavenly Tartine morning bun (made with croissant dough, brown sugar, and orange zest). The line will be long, but it moves fast and it's worth the wait.

MISSION DISTRICT HISTORIC MURALS: Take a walk through this virtual outdoor art gallery, with themes of cultural heritage and social statements in paint, mosaics, and even 3D elements. Start at Balmy Alley (where the murals began in the 1970s), then head to Clarion and Osage Alleys, and finish at the Women's Building on 18th Street, where hundreds of colorful works adorn the walls.

MISSION DELORES PARK: Head to BiRite Creamery and Bakeshop to pick up picnic supplies for an afternoon in Mission Dolores Park filled with glorious hilltop views and the best people watching.

WHAT TO WEAR IN SAN FRANCISCO

The San Francisco girl's vibe is artistic minimalist with curated details, an approach she has down to a science. When planning your San Francisco outfit, think third-piece layering and boots made for walking. What's third-piece layering? Bottoms and top are the first and second pieces, and then the third piece is the extra outfit element—think flannels, kimonos, denim, and long sleeves ... really anything that will keep you cozy when the fog sets in and the temperature drops in late afternoon. In the evening, dress with Edie Sedgwick inspiration—sartorial glam and tormented innocence, a perfectly imperfect aesthetic.

amanda's '70s vibe is so confidently cool!

CAN'T-MISS SAN FRANCISCO

FOR THE FASHIONISTA: Walking distance from Delores Park, you'll find Afterlife. Dig through the T-shirt vault for a Rolling Stones concert T-shirt (if it's your lucky day!) or vintage Levis. Also check out Wallflower Vintage Boutique for more well-curated vintage, Mill Mercantile for luxe basics, Everlane for cashmere layers, and Painted Bird for racks of Instagram-worthy novelty pieces.

FOR THE BIBLIOPHILE: Experience North Beach and the cozy Vesuvio Cafe (a favorite of the beat writers) or Caffe Trieste, home to composers, musicians, and poets. Stop in at Lawrence Ferlinghetti's City Lights Bookstore, a landmark indie bookstore and publisher specializing in world literature and progressive politics.

FOR THE NATURALIST: Take the Golden Gate Bridge to Marin County to visit the quiet waterside neighborhoods. The misty harbor, redwoods, and cliffs have a quiet alchemy just a little way away from the energy of downtown. Visit Sausalito, famous for its community of houseboats. With the fog drifting above, you'll get a sense of how easily Otis Redding found inspiration to write "Sitting on the Dock of the Bay" here.

FOR THE EXPLORER: Travel thirteen miles north of San Francisco to the rustic surfing town of Bolinas. You'll pass organic farm stands, aromatic eucalyptus groves, and then— don't blink because you won't find any street signs (supposedly the locals hide them to keep their homes sacred)—you've arrived. Here you'll find wooden clapboard houses and a peaceful bubble of a town, with a dead end at the ocean. Sunbathe or take a surf lesson, and be sure to check out the graffiti murals lining the beach.

FOR THE MUSIC LOVER: End this flower child adventure back downtown with a show at a one-of-a-kind venue like Bimbo's 365 Club—which boasts red velvet–lined walls, a live mermaid swimming in the lobby, and a nightly burlesque revue; the Chapel—which features soulful and funky touring acts; or the Fillmore (the most famous of them all)—which has hosted thousands of amazing performances from musicians of all genres.

WANDERFUL GIRL: AMANDA BJORN

Photographer / Musician
Los Angeles, CA

AMANDA, photographer and singer in the Los Angeles–based band Bjorn and the Sun, has a soulful awareness—a curiosity for the nostalgic and romantic that shines through in her work. She's created images for Nasty Gal, Urban Outfitters, designer Lykke Wullf, *Cake* magazine, and more that are quietly expressive and often feature models shot in a way that's distinctly different from what we're used to seeing in the standard fashion and beauty ads. Amanda traveled the PCH route with her boyfriend and creative collaborator, David—they ventured up the coastline with a vintage Super 8 camera capturing film for their first folk-rock-meets-soul-pop collection of songs, an EP about the transformation that takes place when you leave everything familiar behind titled *Young and Restless*.

In Amanda's Bag:

My grandfather's
Rolleiflex camera!

"I love California's physical vastness, cultural diversity, and its light. You can be anything and everything you want here. The idea of a road trip was crucial to the songs we created, so when we were thinking of making music videos for those songs, we wanted to capture that essence of movement by traveling ourselves. For our song "Blue" we envisioned filming along the California coast, so we brought along our old school Super 8 camera, packed up my car, and headed north."

CHAPTER

Two.

FLORIDA COASTIN'

POP-ART PASTELS, dynamite Art Deco architecture, and a salty wildness are what's in store on this route. Florida has a good-looking confidence that begins with the people and extends to an atmosphere of perfectly harmonized fun times, making it deserving of the moniker "the Sunshine State." The cities we will visit have a cotton-candy sweetness coupled with an eighties New Wave vibe topped off with fireworks (literally) in the sky. The beaches are a visual tour of bright whites, crystal blues, and golden tropics.

sunkissed and sandy

THE MODERN MERMAID

THE MODERN MERMAID is playful and flirtatious. She's an island explorer who plans the best beach bonfire bashes and falls in love while skinny-dipping under the full moon. She travels with a "no boys allowed" rule because she'd never pass up a getaway with her best girls. She relies on dresses, playsuits, and rompers—garments that are outfits in themselves—because she loves easy-to-wear pieces that elevate her resort-chic style. The Florida girl believes Audrey Hepburn's famous adage that "happy girls are the prettiest girls," and the Sunshine State has the happiest girls around.

SHE WAS THE GIRL WHO BIT THE HORIZON. THE ONE WHO PEELED THE STARS FROM THE SKY AND PUT THEM ON HER TONGUE. SHE WAS THE GIRL WHO WAS HUNGRY FOR THE ENTIRE UNIVERSE; THE ONE WHO CRAVED THE TASTE OF MAGIC.
—D. ANTOINETTE FOY

the modern mermaid
CAPSULE WARDROBE

For surf chasing and day-to-night dance parties

Silk chiffon crop tops and matching flare-leg trousers

Printed playsuits in floral and stripe motifs

Hand-stitched halter bikinis and off-the-shoulder ruffled tops

Oversize sweatshirts for layering

For beach bonfires and slumber parties

Embroidered tunic and caftan-style cover-ups

Quirky kimonos in a variety of prints

A mix of triangle tops and one-piece bathing suits paired with cutoff denim

Footwear and accessories

Statement jewels and watches

Hand-painted straw clutches

Oversize wide brim hats

Round, cat-eye, and wayfarer sunglasses

Strands of Deco-inspired chains

Metallic gladiator sandals

Lace-up leather booties

Vintage roller skates

Turban-style hair wraps

For music-loving midnight queens

Chambray jumpsuits

Slinky, swing dresses

Graphic T-shirt dresses to layer over swimwear

the modern mermaid

LOVES...

MOVIES: *Blue Crush* (2002), *The Blue Lagoon* (1980), *Easy to Love* (1953), *Great Expectations* (1998), *Where the Boys Are* (1960), *Stranger Than Paradise* (1984), *The Beach* (2000), *The Truman Show* (1998), *Rock of Ages* (2012), *Miami Vice* (2006)

READS: *Miami* (Joan Didion), *The Blue Lagoon* (Henry De Vere Stacpoole), *Kate Spade New York: Places to Go, People to See* (Kate Spade), *Tourist Season* (Carl Hiaasen), *Beaches* (Gray Malin), and check out the current bestseller list for popular beach reads

BANDS: Bananarama, Frank Sinatra, Phoenix, Haim, the Miami Sound Machine, Jimmy Buffett, First Aid Kit, Melody's Echo Chamber, Tennis

FLORIDA COASTIN' VIBES PLAYLIST:

▶ "Sunny Afternoon" (The Kinks)

▶ "Kokomo" (The Beach Boys)

▶ "No Scrubs" (TLC)

▶ "Cicadas and Gulls" (Feist)

▶ "Welcome to Miami" (Will Smith)

▶ "Lucky Star" (Madonna)

▶ "Rhythm Is Gonna Get You" (Gloria Estefan & Miami Sound Machine)

▶ "Wish You Were Here" (Pink Floyd)

▶ "Sweet Life" (Frank Ocean)

▶ "Walcott" (Vampire Weekend)

THE ROUTE

THE FREE-SPIRITED WANDERER: Millions of people visit Florida every year and never see much past the interstate, theme parks, and cruise ship billboards. This is your chance to really see the sights. Your trip begins in Miami, travels up Florida's Turnpike to Orlando, and then ends at the beaches of route 30A.

THE LONG WEEKENDER: Traveling by car, you can make a long weekend of Miami and Orlando (or choose just one and explore thoroughly!). You can also fly directly to the Northwest Florida Beaches International Airport and take a slow drive along the beaches of route 30A.

THE DAY(S) TRIPPER: Pick your vibe (and one spot): Miami's energy, Orlando's kitsch, or the beachy renewal of route 30A.

MIAMI, FL

Miami is cleverly referred to as the "American Riviera." Take one step on its white sand beaches and you'll realize why: The luxury of the pastel-colored buildings brings to mind the glamour of old Hollywood and visions of a 1940s Rita Hayworth or Frank Sinatra and his crew dressed to the nines.

Miami is the only major US city founded by a woman (#GirlPower!) and the city is a melting pot of people from all over the world. It is a laid-back metropolis of good food and fashion. (In fact, my first solo road trip ever was a drive to Miami for a few days of vintage hunting. A lasting love of vintage Gucci, Louis Vuitton, and Missoni was born that weekend.)

TWO DAYS IN MIAMI

FREEHAND MIAMI: Stay at the Freehand, a luxury hostel—it's the epitome of laid-back cool with a summer camp vibe. Sip Miller High Life in brown bags and play a round of bocce ball in the lush backyard with backpackers and locals alike.

beach bound with spf slathered on thick!

WHAT TO WEAR IN MIAMI

Miami gallerinas wear monochromatic graphic looks and all-white separates, indie-style mavens are in glitter eyeliner and Frida Kahlo headwear, and street artists and musicians don skater shoes and layers of denim. When the sun goes down, throw on a sheer printed mini shirt dress over your crocheted monokini, add shimmering sandals and statement jewelry, and you're set!

ART DECO DISTRICT: Start your morning with a café con leche or a cortadito and find a spot to simply watch the locals in their element. Walk along Ocean Drive and Collins Avenue to soak in the architecture of the retro-fabulous hotels. At once nostalgic and new, their exteriors boast geometric shapes and faded pastels, while the interiors are full of sleek curves, shiny chrome, and gleaming terrazzo floors—every hotel is absolute eye candy.

LINCOLN ROAD FLEA MARKET: If you arrive on the weekend, the Sunday flea market on Lincoln Road is filled with vendors selling little baubles and trinkets. Once you've filled your bag with treasures to take home, take a stroll down Lincoln Road to experience some of the best shopping anywhere.

ALCHEMIST: The flagship location of this boutique, a storefront in a parking deck on Lincoln Road, is a sensory dream: foam walls, pulsating film projections as a backdrop, and designer garments and jewels from it-girl fashion lines like Alaïa, Marni, Isabel Marant, and The Row.

BASE: A lifestyle retail pioneer, BASE Superstore appeals to a specific "Tribe," according to the owner who personally curates the super-hip selection of goods. With art-gallery-meets-music-bar vibes, BASE has its own vending machine at the Mondrian South Beach Hotel and an outpost at the Delano Hotel.

LITTLE HAVANA: After shopping, take the 20-minute drive to Calle Ocho, the main drag of Little Havana, where fruit stands, coffee windows (or *ventanitas*), art galleries, and Afro-Cuban beat music keep things lively. The Cuban culture permeates—here you'll find colorful murals, cigar rollers deeply engrossed in their work, and the bustle of local activity and tourists exploring. On a recent trip, we stopped at Domino Park to watch a little old lady in pink and green sponge curlers make some moves on her elderly gentlemen playing partners.

sunny days in little havana

BOOKS & BOOKS: A few minutes away is the shop Joan Didion once wandered through while writing her book *Miami*. This literary community favorite is Miami's most legendary bookstore. The poetry section is awe-inspiring, as is the collection of art and fashion-specific coffee table books.

CAN'T-MISS MIAMI

FOR THE ART AFICIONADO: Head over to Wynwood, comprised of art complexes, galleries, performing art spaces, eclectic restaurants, cafés, and one of the largest open-air mural installations in the world. The art district, which is likely the most Instagrammed neighborhood in Miami, is also a mecca for fashion.

FOR THE FASHIONISTA: Always a step ahead of the trends, shop at Style Mafia—another Wynwood destination and serious favorite of Miami's fashion set. Style Mafia offers a collection of pieces coming in at under $200. You can also pick up hand-embroidered Mexican tunics at the neighborhood's Malaquita Design and find delicately crafted baubles at Boho Hunter.

FOR THE NIGHT OWL: The Miami nightlife scene is ferocious—clubs never close and there's a new hot spot every week. For a low-key night, head to Gramps and enjoy their "famous air-conditioning" and cold beer while the DJ spins a vinyl set. For a more upbeat experience, dance until sunrise at the Electric Pickle Co. or Wood. (If you make it to Wood on a Tuesday, be sure to take advantage of the free "Taco Tuesday" tacos!) In the morning, recover with a cold-pressed juice at Jugofresh and a coffee at specialty-roaster Panther Coffee.

FOR THE MUSIC LOVER: Indie music fans should skip the clubs and dive in deep for local music of the small venue variety. Hit Bardot (there's no sign, and no social media-ing from inside) or Churchill's Pub after a day of frolicking in the surf to hear top-notch local music. Shop women-owned Sweat Records' one-dollar bin, and explore their massive selection of music of all genres.

Leaving from Miami, our next stop is Orlando.

Florida's Turnpike, Miami to Orlando (approx. 230 miles, 3.5 hours)

ORLANDO, FL

Like jelly shoes and babydoll dresses, you're never too old for a touch of Disney princess magic with your best girls. In recent years, Disney has been having a major fashion moment. With collaborations with brands like Lazy Oaf, A Bathing Ape (a streetwear brand out of Japan that your hip little brother definitely knows about), and Coach, the American classic, Mickey is on the style map like never before.

IF YOU CAN DREAM IT, YOU CAN DO IT. —WALT DISNEY

keiko as minnie mouse (but she loves snow white, too!)

71

Disney is the ultimate representation of American pop culture, and Mickey Mouse is a classic American icon. So, when in Rome (or Florida), we have to make a pit stop at the happiest place on Earth.

A few years ago, my best friend proposed the idea of meeting me at the airport as I returned from a trip abroad . . . but not at my home airport. Her idea? We'd meet in Orlando, have a Disney pajama party, pay Mickey a visit, and then road trip home. I was in.

Inspired by that magical sleepover, this short detour is kitsch-central. Grab your best girlfriend and pack matching outfits with a Disney theme: Minnie overalls, vintage graphic Mickey Ts, and maybe even a princess bow, pearl earrings, and polka-dot bangles. If you don't have something already, you can score some colorful Mickey gear at any hotel convenience store or gift shop.

DISNEY IN A DAY

To successfully conquer Disney in a day, you have to map out your plan. Pick a Buena Vista motel that offers shuttle service to the park and free parking. This is the time to use online booking sites—find whatever resort-type motel is offering a deal and choose that. (I won't make that recommendation again, but for Disney, it's your best bet.)

Install the app that gives the wait times at your favorite rides, and be sure to be on the first shuttle in the morning. If you play it right, you can hit Space Mountain, Splash Mountain, Thunder Mountain, the Mad Tea Party, It's A Small World, and the Haunted Mansion by noon. After lunch at the Tomorrowland Terrace, cool off with a Dole Whip, spend some time snapping selfies at Cinderella's Castle, and either hit the road, or, if you've got the time, hang around to catch the Wishes fireworks display over the castle in the evening. Day passes are right at $100 (and doing a day of Disney with your bestie will be 100 percent worth it).

Next stop: the beaches of route 30A.

Orlando to Highway 98 to Scenic 30A's Rosemary Beach (approx. 135 miles, 3 hours)

ACTUALLY, THE BEST GIFT YOU COULD HAVE GIVEN HER WAS A LIFETIME OF ADVENTURES…
—LEWIS CARROLL

BEACHES OF 30A, FL

30A, the nickname given to Scenic Highway 30A, is a dreamscape beach nirvana. A twenty-five-mile corridor that rises and falls along the coastline of northwest Florida, the drive offers up sugar-white sand beaches and rare coastal dune lakes nestled along sea oat–covered hills. Juxtaposed against pine forests and marshlands, it's an eco-adventurer's wonderland. Keep driving along, and eventually you'll run into the charming little beach towns of 30A tucked into the landscape.

I MUST BE A MERMAID. I HAVE NO FEAR OF DEPTHS AND A GREAT FEAR OF SHALLOW LIVING.
—ANAÏS NIN

beach party!

WHAT TO WEAR TO THE BEACHES OF 30A

30A caters to the girl who always has a towel stashed in her jeep, sunscreen in her glovebox, and a bikini in her bag. She has a polaroid collage of vintage surfboards and has a perpetual Coppertone tan. She's watched her favorite movie, *The Blue Lagoon*, at least a hundred times. 30A days can range from boardwalk afternoons to breezy beach bonfires, so it's best to start with your favorite bikini and prepare to layer as the day goes. You can travel to all four of the beaches in a day, or spend the whole time cozying up in one. But no matter which beach you choose, your bathing suit, your favorite sunnies, and a pair of sandals to go from the beach to the boardwalk are all you need.

Most 30A first-timers comment that they never knew America had such beaches—they'd maybe traveled to Hawaii or to the Southern Caribbean thinking those were the only places they'd find white sandscapes and emerald waters like these. It's interesting that these Florida beaches have been on numerous "best of" lists and somehow still manage to be a secret. The architecture here is a blend of eclectic Caribbean styles, including old Florida's traditional multistory homes and cottages with white picket fences mixed with new urban-style retreats.

Our trip has you traveling east to west to visit Rosemary Beach, Alys Beach, Seaside, and Grayton Beach. Here's the lowdown on each.

TWO DAYS ON 30A

ROSEMARY BEACH
Old World European village meets small-town hospitality.

Rent a bike and go play on the sprawling green lawn where the beach meets the Pearl Hotel. The boardwalk promenades and secluded pathways that wind between the carriage houses and cottages give Rosemary an idyllic charm. The Pearl is the place to stay—with sun-drenched terraces and poolside cabanas, it has a West-Indies-meets-Hemingway's-Cuba feel. In the town

center you'll find there's a little of everything: candy and coffee shops, wine bars, restaurants, and boutiques.

Shop at Ophelia Swimwear, owned by the consummate gypsy girl, Tori Pickren Von Hoene. The Ophelia girl is a firecracker: a carefree fun-loving sun chaser. With several locations, the shops are each stocked with brands like Beach Riot, Frankie's, Mikoh, and Boys and Arrows. Stop in to meet Tori; she's the petite beach babe with the biggest smile in town.

ALYS BEACH

Harmonious new-urban luxury and impeccable cool.

Alys Beach is a vision of white-hot architecture and iconic palm trees with courtyard homes and villas featuring Bermudan-style design. Upon arrival, pick up fresh donuts at Charlie's Donut Truck and a coffee at the cozy Fonville Press. Visit Alys Shoppe for leather accessories from local brand Coastal Road and peruse the event calendar for trunk shows from design stars like Christian Siriano.

Spend a few moments meditating on the beachfront bluffs rising several stories above the Gulf Ocean waters. Look for the monarch butterflies fluttering along, heading south for the winter.

SEASIDE

Picket-fence Truman Show *meets Airstream party.*

There are three main places to hang out in Seaside: the beach, the town center, which is the central hub of all of 30A, and then the Ruskin Place artist colony, which originated as a workshop district with artisans living above their workspaces surrounding sculpture-filled Fairy Park.

The vintage Airstream food trucks parked on the main drag anchor the town center. There's gourmet grilled cheese sandwiches, fresh-squeezed juices, ball-park-style hot dogs, and more. Across the street sits Perspicasity, an outdoor market inspired by the breezy open-air bohemian bazaars of Europe. Opened in 1981 as a fruit stand, the huts by the sea offer tie-dyed caftans, hand-batiked maxis, Italian leather sandals, and all the supplies you'll need for a glam day of poolside lounging.

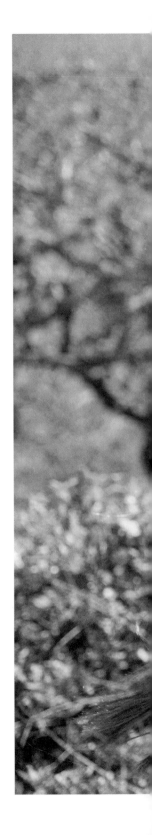

Visit Central Square Records for odds and ends and the newest vinyl releases, and pick up picnic supplies at gourmet grocer Modica Market.

At night, score a veranda table at Bud & Alley's or their neighboring Bud & Alley's Pizza Bar. Opened three decades ago by a couple of twenty-four-year-old surfing buddies, and named for a cat and dog roaming around town, the unpretentious eateries have fresh local seafood and to-die-for artisanal cheese pizzas.

GRAYTON BEACH
As free-spirited and quirky as the unofficial town motto: "Nice Dogs, Strange People."

One of the oldest beach towns in the South, Grayton's laid-back feel effervesces from its funky little community. Rent a historic beach cottage or a Grayton Beach Park cabin for around $100, and make friends with the locals for a jeep ride or a night of bonfires on the beach. Both are allowed by permit, and there are even companies that will handle bonfire building for you.

Shop the Monet Monet Maker's Market, an open-air market located in a community home and garden inspired by Monet's residence in Giverny, France. The market features artists and local designers including Nicole Paloma, a longtime favorite of the 30A boho glamour girls. Stop into Grayton Beach Gypsea for a mix of resort- and bohemian-chic-style dresses and separates. If you're looking for kimonos and fringe on a budget or a locally made trinket to take home, this shop has plenty of options.

Hike the mesmerizing dunes and pine flatwoods of the two-thousand-acre Grayton Beach Park. Drop in to Chiringo for a late lunch and the specialty, Agua de Valencia.

End the Florida Coastin' days with a girls' night out: Either dine and dance at Pandora's, an old-school steakhouse and lounge, or catch local favorite Dread Clampitt doing "St. James Infirmary Blues" at the bohemian-style beach shack the Red Bar. You'll head home wrapped in your beautiful summer tan remembering that friendship and a sandy bathing suit is sometimes all you really need.

WANDERFUL GIRL: KAYLYN WEIR

Creative Entrepreneur
Seaside, FL

WHEN KAYLYN'S NOT bouncing around the surf in her heart-shaped sunnies, the pink-haired beauty is running her creative studio where she puts together branding campaigns for small businesses. She's a favorite of the "girl gang" over at LA design house ban.do—they adore her all-pink-everything style so much that they flew her and her bestie to LA for a #havefunphotoshoot! Kaylyn considers Highway 30A to be heaven on earth; she decided after vacationing along these beaches for years that she had to make it her forever home. Wanderful girls know how to turn vacation vibes into a lifestyle, and Kaylyn's got that down to a science.

In Kaylyn's Bag:

My rose water facial spray and peppermint chapstick!

"We all cherish classic beach moments—sand in your shoes, the smell of salt-filled air, a constant echo of reggae music, and happy hours where colorful daiquiris are never served without paper umbrellas. You can find all of that here, but the reason I love 30A most is the unique beach communities, each with their own 'swagger.' From Airstream restaurants that line Main Street to coastal dune lakes to rows of pastel beach cottages, this place is so much more than the infamous airbrushed T-shirts that seem to accompany every beach scene. Everywhere you go, the Southern spirit of 'hello' is infectious."

CHAPTER

Three.

THE EASTERN SEABOARD

LANDMARK LIGHTHOUSES, seaside salt-box cottages, and rustic one-room lobster shacks are just a few of the highlights of this idyllic New England journey. Rocky inlets and seaside forests line the charming drive through the lands where America's most glamorous royal family, the Kennedys, vacationed. This is a trip for taking out the beach cruiser bicycles by day and cozying up at night with a gigantic blanket and a fire. For our trip, we'll be traveling up Highway 1, departing from New York, and traveling along the Eastern Seaboard of Maine for a quintessential all-American road trip.

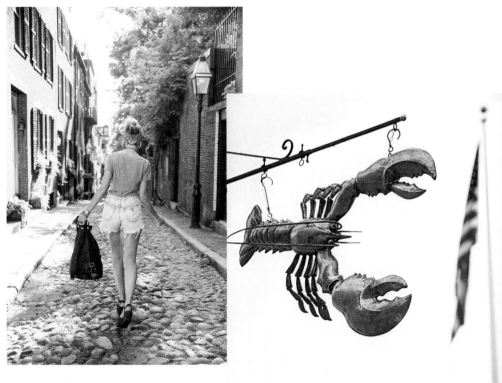

*lobster shacks and
cobblestone strolls*

THE SEASIDE STAR

THE SEASIDE STAR lives in vibrant head wrap scarves, oversize cat-eye sunglasses, and shift dresses à la Jackie O. She plays croquet out on the lush backyard lawn and loves dressing up with her girlfriends in decadent vintage finds. She believes a girl is never too old for a tea party and loves those forever-young moments on these nostalgia-driven roads.

IT'S A FUNNY THING COMING HOME. NOTHING CHANGES. EVERYTHING LOOKS THE SAME, FEELS THE SAME, EVEN SMELLS THE SAME. YOU REALIZE WHAT'S CHANGED IS YOU.
—F. SCOTT FITZGERALD

the seaside star
CAPSULE WARDROBE

For lobster shacks and bonfire nights

A stack of 1960s printed smock dresses

High-waisted scalloped shorts

Polka-dot prints in modern silhouettes

For cobblestone street strolling

Classic monochromatic T-shirts

Breton sweaters and striped button downs

Boyfriend jeans or cutoffs

Oversize varsity sweaters for layering

Footwear and accessories

Cat-eye sunglasses

Cross-body purses and skinny belts in primary colors

Silk-printed turban head scarves

Leather ballet flats and slides

Neckerchiefs in a variety of colors

Wide-brim hats

Minimalist diamond studs

Architectural cuffs

For afternoons on the lawn

Bold, geometric-printed separates

A lace-embellished wrap dress

Off-the-shoulder tops

Novelty prints with peter pan collars

the seaside star

LOVES...

MOVIES: *Moonrise Kingdom* (2012), *Message in a Bottle* (1999), *High Society* (1956), *The Royal Tenenbaums* (2001), *The Thomas Crown Affair* (1968), *The Little Girl Who Lives Down the Lane* (1976), *Clue* (1985), *One Crazy Summer* (1986), *The Witches of Eastwick* (1987)

READS: *Kate Spade New York: All in Good Taste* (Kate Spade), *The Official Preppy Handbook* (Lisa Birnbach), *Revolutionary Road* (Richard Yates), *Happy Times* (Lee Radziwill), *Jackie After O* (Tina Cassidy), *Take Ivy* (Shosuke Ishizu)

BANDS: Passion Pit, James Taylor, The Pixies, Norah Jones, Lana Del Rey, Simon & Garfunkel, Vampire Weekend, Bob Dylan

EASTERN SEABOARD VIBES PLAYLIST:

▶ "Time to Pretend" (MGMT)

▶ "Walk on the Ocean" (Toad the Wet Sprocket)

▶ "Castles in the Sand" (Stevie Wonder)

▶ "Old Cape Cod" (The Norman Petty Trio)

▶ "Sleeping In" (The Postal Service)

▶ "Summertime" (The Head and the Heart)

▶ "Life in a Northern Town" (Dream Academy)

▶ "Cape Cod Kwassa Kwassa" (Vampire Weekend)

▶ "Tangled Up in Blue" (Bob Dylan)

THE ROUTE

THE FREE-SPIRITED WANDERER: Arrive via plane into New York City and begin your drive up 95 North or 1 North. Once you've crossed state lines into Connecticut, take 1 North up through Old Saybrook and continue north to Boston. Alternatively, you can arrive via plane to Boston, considered the gateway to New England, and begin the trip there. From Boston, the trip is a leisurely drive up the southern coast of Maine.

THE LONG WEEKENDER: Start in Boston and head north to Kennebunkport and Portland. Spend a night or two in each town along the way.

THE DAY(S) TRIPPER: Choose one destination and spend all of your time there. Travel into either Boston or Portland and pick one of the coastal Maine destinations.

For longer trips, we'll assume a start in New York because it has the most flight options. If you can make time to spend a day in the city, there are so many ways to fill it. But for this trip, we're heading directly to Old Saybrook.

OLD SAYBROOK, CT

The stretch along Highway 1 crossing into Connecticut is a seaside spectacle. Yachts and million-dollar vacationers' retreats line
the shore. Once you've made your way up to Old Saybrook—
where Katharine Hepburn famously summered "in paradise"—
the towns become distinctly sleepier as the formality fades away.

one of everything, please!

yum!

Take a detour down to the Harbor One Marina in Old Saybrook
for lunch at Liv's Shack. Order the Connecticut-style buttered
lobster roll—it's overstuffed with fresh-from-the-shell chunks
and will be a personal favorite of this entire road trip, guar-
anteed. Get a side of hand-cut fries and find a spot out on the
porch to watch the seagulls play.

Get back on the road and head north. Next stopover will be
Boston.

*Old Saybrook, Connecticut, to Boston, Massachusetts, I-95 N
+ 1 N (approx. 130 miles, 2–3 hours)*

BOSTON, MA

Once you arrive in Boston, head straight to Beacon Hill. Beacon Hill is a charming little neighborhood full of adorable shops, brownstones, and townhouses. A trip to Boston is worth it, if for nothing else but window shopping along Charles Street and a meal.

BOSTON IN AN AFTERNOON

CHARLES STREET: A short distance from the big brands lining the famous Newbury Street, Charles Street is full of almost exclusively independently owned boutiques. Pop into Good for delicately unique luxuries and understated accessories, Crush Boutique for fashion-forward lines like House of Harlow and Alice & Olivia, and December Thieves for locally sourced treasures.

ACORN STREET: Teeter along the cobblestone-paved Acorn Street, home to nineteenth-century row houses of artisans and craftspeople. Snap plenty of photos—Acorn Street is rumored to be the most photographed street in the country. From there, wander the narrow side streets throughout the neighborhood over to the prestigious addresses of Louisburg Square to see the Greek statues and the home of author Louisa May Alcott.

The New England coast is full of authentic seafood dishes and restaurants. After a few hours of shopping, stop at the Island Creek Oyster Bar at the Hotel Commonwealth to enjoy the raw bar before getting back on the road. Opened by a bunch of super-cool guys who revived an abandoned oyster farm down in Duxbury, it's a great place to get a fantastic farm-to-table meal in a laid-back atmosphere before heading north.

Boston, Massachusetts, to York Harbor, Maine, on US-1 (approx. 75 miles, 2 hours)

WHAT TO WEAR IN BOSTON

Boston girls embrace scholastic style: clean lines, stripes, and neutrals with a sporty-chic influence. The modern bohemian in Boston adds her own flair with statement accessories and cool retro finds. If you're traveling in the colder months, pack a down-filled or faux-fur coat, snow boots, and a shearling pom-pom beanie.

YORK HARBOR, ME

Crossing the state line, Highway 1 hugs the coastline of Maine's classic New England scenery and then dips off into marshlands and fragrant forests. Summer nights in Maine are cool, so be sure your weekender is packed with sweaters (in red, white, and blue, of course). If you're traveling in the fall and winter, you'll need to be prepared with warm outerwear from Barbour and vintage Burberry.

Starting in York Harbor and ending at our farthest northern point of Portland, our destinations are all considered "southern" Maine. A note here about that: Touring the Maine Coast is an extraordinary journey—including the tidal inlets, Maine has more coastline than California! It's larger than the other five New England states combined—17 million acres in full. To travel from the southernmost point up to Canada would truly take weeks, so we focused on a few charmingly southern towns.

maine!

Get off Highway 1 at the hip little hamlet of Kittery, about fifteen minutes south of York Harbor. Travel down scenic 103 all the way to the harbor, and drop your L.L. Bean Boat and Tote bag at the York Harbor Inn. The York Harbor Inn is a collection of historic properties including the Chapman Cottage, a gorgeously renovated summer home named for socialite Fanny Chapman. Have dinner on the porch at the Tavern at Chapman Cottage or descend below deck at the Inn's main building to the Ship's Cellar Pub for a few predinner drinks. You'll feel certain you've boarded a fancified schooner.

Before continuing the cruise north, don't miss a visit to snap a few photos on the Wiggly Bridge on Lilac Lane. It's known to be the world's smallest suspension bridge and, yes, it wiggles under your feet while crossing.

Between the villages of York Harbor and York Beach, stop for ice cream at any of the dozen or so stands lining Long Sands Beach. The beach here offers a view of the Nubble Lighthouse, which sits high on the edge of a rocky peninsula dotted with colonial clapboard homes.

York Harbor, Maine, to Kennebunkport, Maine, on US-1 (approx. 20 miles, 40 minutes)

KENNEBUNKPORT, ME

This picturesque harbor town with a river running through it is full of effervescent charm. Settled in the 1600s as a ship-building mecca, Kennebunkport became a resort destination as sea captains built fine mansions, many of which are preserved today.

KENNEBUNKPORT IN A DAY

KENNEBUNK'S LOWER VILLAGE AND DOCK SQUARE: Wear your boater hat and saturated, tailored separates to shop along the Kennebunk River, full of boutiques, galleries, books, antique shops, and waterfront cafés. Pick up a tourmaline gemstone mined in Maine at Coastal Jewelers or something for your home at Good Earth Pottery Gallery.

THE "WEDDING CAKE" HOUSE: Stop to take photos at this local attraction. During our visit, a jeep full of local teenage boys pulled up, shouting, "There's nothing to see, it's just a house!" But one look and you'll realize that this landmark would never be considered "just a house." Don't miss it.

NUNAN'S LOBSTER HUT: Drive along Ocean Avenue for dinner at this family-owned establishment, which has served dinner the same way every night since 1953. The seafood is fresh, locally caught, and cooked to order—the epitome of the perfect lobster shack.

THE CAPTAIN JEFFERDS INN: Check in at this historic inn, which was once a sea captain's home. Rent a cruiser bicycle from the innkeeper and take off for a late afternoon beach ride. In the early evening, the inn's sunroom is a perfect place for a proper ladies tea party. Or, buy a bottle of champagne from the inn's stock and slip into something glamorous for a Gatsby-style girls' night in.

In the morning, breakfast is communal and complimentary in the formal dining room, with offerings like peach shortcake and Maine blueberry–stuffed French toast. After breakfast, pack up and head north to one of the few working waterfronts left in the country, Portland.

Kennebunkport to Portland, State Route 9 E and US-1 N (approx. 30 miles, 1 hour)

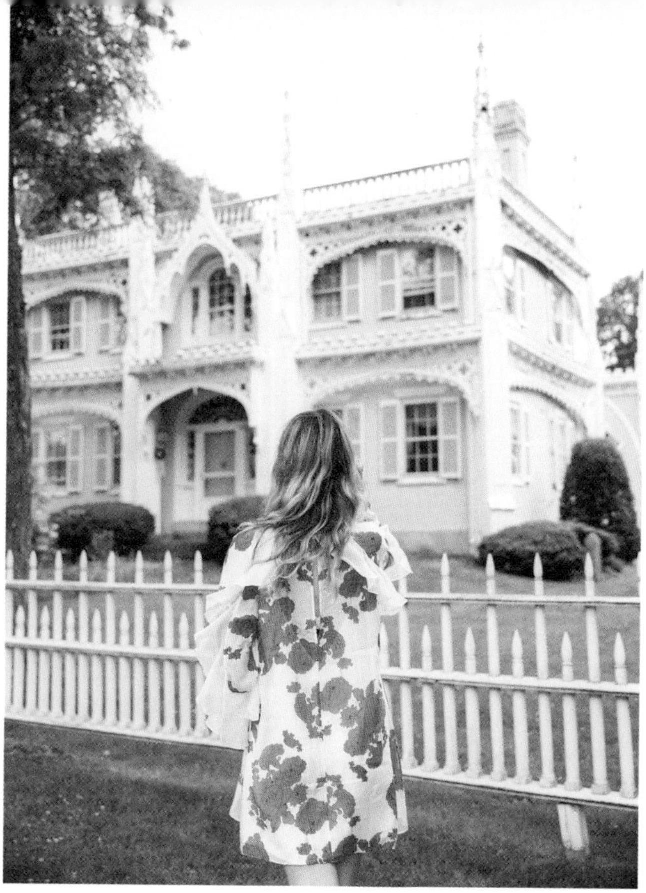

nothing to see here!

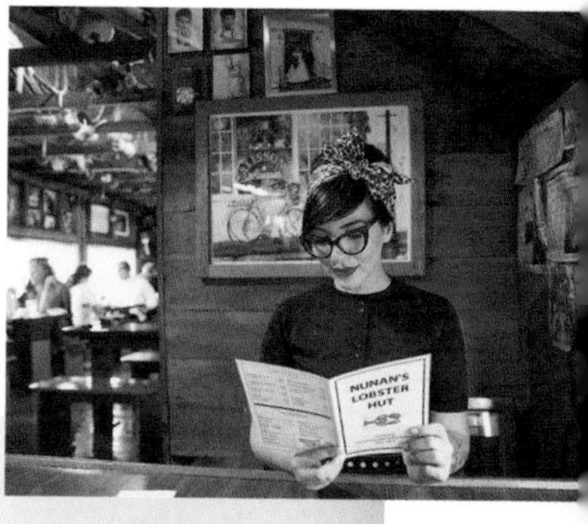

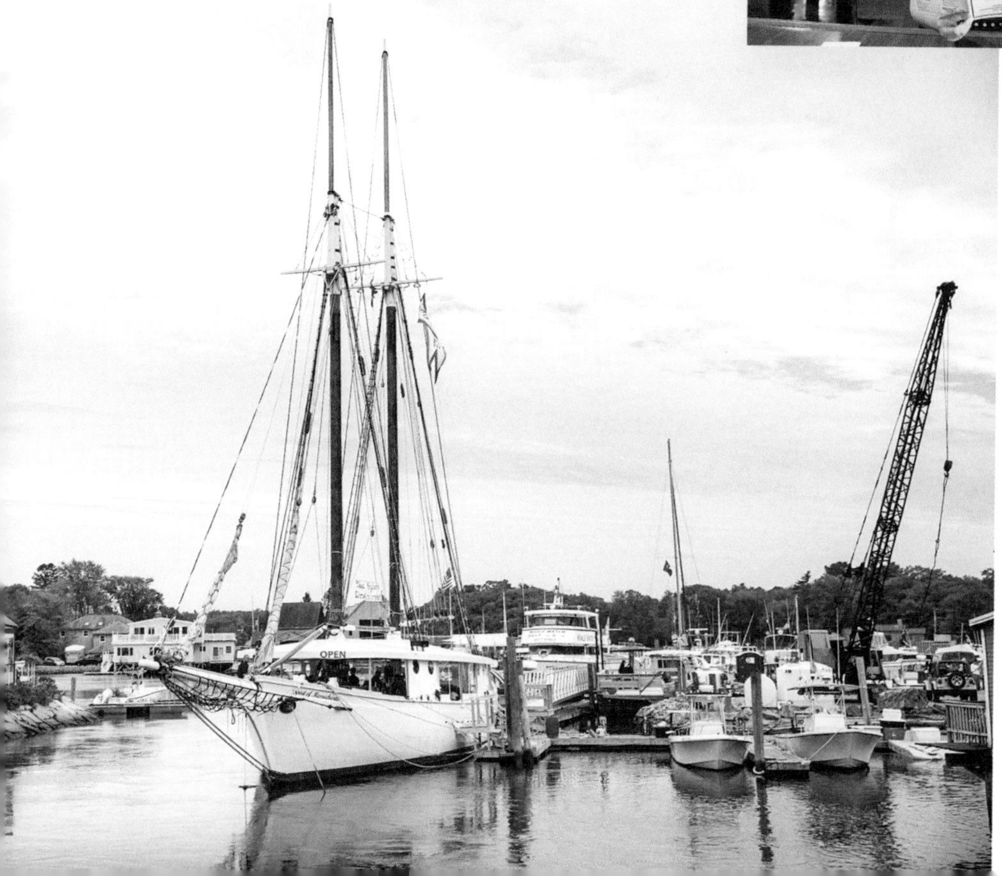

PORTLAND, ME

Portland is a laid-back, youthful place catering to craftspeople and fishermen alike. It's a city where apothecaries like Portland General Store, which crafts organic, vegan, and vintage-inspired grooming essentials, thrive, and restaurants like Eventide Oyster Co. redefine the local classics. Portland is Maine's largest city, but it's quaint compared to the usual standards—the Old Port and the Arts District can both be covered easily on foot.

WHAT TO WEAR IN PORTLAND

Portland girls have an imaginative eccentricity about them— their style is quite a departure from their New England counter-parts. Quirky tea-length dresses, ruffled shorts, and blouses are perfect for the mild spring and summer months. In the winter, the Portland girl layers distressed grandpa sweaters, thick wool tights, and wellie boots or stacked-sole Mary Janes with her cat-eye sunglasses.

TWO DAYS IN PORTLAND

INN BY THE SEA: Arrive into Cape Elizabeth's eco-luxury inn, ten miles east of downtown Portland. Of every property recommended on these road trips, the Inn has the highest average price point; however, the environmental preservation efforts and the wild, unspoiled feel make it the perfect place for a nomadic girl with "private princess" Carolyn Bessette vibes. I recommend spending two days at the Inn to fully enjoy it.

MAXWELL'S FARM: In the afternoon pick strawberries at the farm directly next to the Inn. Ask for a lesson on the flora all along Cape Elizabeth from the Inn's gardener before venturing into downtown. The surrounding indigenous gardens are a resplendent habitat for wildlife and home to a growing population of New England cottontails, a type of rabbit that recently approached the endangered list.

PORTLAND OBSERVATORY: Travel over to Munjoy Hill, bordered on three sides by Casco Bay, the Fore River, and Back Cove to the Portland Observatory. Take the ten-dollar tour to revel in the breathtaking views and receive a fascinating history lesson at America's last standing maritime signal tower.

CAN'T-MISS PORTLAND

FOR THE VINTAGE DEVOTEE: Visit the splendidly curated inventory of vintage and thrift finds at the shops throughout the city. Find is great for denim overalls and faux-fur jackets, and the favorite of our trip, Moody Lords, has stacks of 1960s-era swing dresses for less than thirty dollars each.

FOR THE INTERIORS AFICIONADO: Portland Architectural Salvage has repurposed and discarded relics that have made the pages of Design*Sponge and *Green Builder* magazine.

FOR THE HISTORY BUFF: En route to downtown sits the Portland Head Light. It's Maine's oldest lighthouse, home to the infamous ghost bride, Lydia Carver. Residents share stories of her friendly spirit wandering the beaches in her wedding dress. (The Eastern Seaboard girl, a romantic soul, lives for stories like these.)

trying every
lobster roll in town

Moody
Lords
Vintage

FOR THE FASHIONISTA: Portland Flea-for-All features stylish wares from vendors ranging from Blood & Whiskey Studio (unique hand-printed shirts) to Honeyscout (handmade semiprecious and raw mineral jewelry).

Before you depart, take a leisurely stroll along the wharf or the beach boardwalk and promise your traveling partner you'll be back basking in that golden Northeastern light next year, just like the Kennedys would have done.

WANDERFUL GIRL: KEIKO LYNN GROVES

Style Ambassador /
Makeup Artist
Brooklyn, NY

KEIKO IS TRULY one of the OG style bloggers. She shared stories of her eclectic style, her love for animals (she has three adopted cats and an adorable pup, Miku), and brilliantly detailed makeup tutorials via Open Diary and Live Journal a decade before fashion bloggers started sitting front row at fashion week. Her style has always been authentically her own—inspired by clothing her grandmother taught her to make and vintage styles paired with indie designer finds. She's the girl to look to for inspiration when packing for a road trip: She makes getting dressed in the morning joyful, and doesn't everyone want to travel with a girl that exudes happiness through her style? I'm lucky to call her a friend and to have had her along on our tour of New England, sharing her unique approach to packing in style.

In Keiko's Bag:

My Pomeranian eskimo unicorn, Miku!

"For our New England road trip, Americana reds, whites, and blues (with the occasional pastel) found their way into my suitcase. Although I always stay true to my own style, I love following some sort of theme when traveling, whether it's a color story or an overall vibe. It's not about fitting in— or even standing out, for that matter—it's about having fun with the entire experience, from start to finish. Packing with the destination in mind is part of the adventure!"

CHAPTER

Four.

THE TEXAS HIDEAWAYS

sampson,
the guard
donkey ♡

ON THIS JOURNEY, we'll have wigwams and ancient cattle skulls juxtaposed with wildflowers and ravens circling overhead. Make this trip with someone close to your heart; the Texas roads can be lonely—a soliloquy to metamorphic skies shifting from pastels to deep blues depending on the time of day and which direction the wind is blowing. We begin in Austin, the "live music capital," home to SXSW and Austin City Limits, and a creative entrepreneurs' hub—Facebook, Google, and Apple all have offices here. As we continue into southwest Texas, Marfa and Terlingua offer up a different type of creative collective: With few conventional nine-to-fivers, these Mexican border towns are an artistic utopia, offering stone-cold silence like so many desert towns. However, there's also a vibrant cultural community drawn to the inspiration and transient lifestyle here.

This trip holds a special place in my heart. It was my first true desert road trip, and I felt a deep magic in its wildness. It's a place to get lost—figuratively, of course—in the vastness of this great big country.

THE ELECTRIC COWGIRL

THE DESERT-DWELLING girl is down-to-earth and full of lively artistic ambition. She has glowing skin and often unkempt hair, her style a nod to youthful 1970s summers. West Texas is all about extremes: blistering heat in the summers and stark white cold in the winter. She dresses as if she's the muse for an artist or designer inspired by both old westerns and Jetson-like futuristic space films. She wears casual sequins and sparkles paired with breezy, breathable fabrics. She's conquered the art of dressing for the elements, piling on bundles of textured layers to ward off chilly evening air.

LOVE IS THE ULTIMATE OUTLAW. IT JUST WON'T ADHERE TO ANY RULES. THE MOST ANY OF US CAN DO IS TO SIGN ON AS ITS ACCOMPLICE. —TIM ROBBINS, EVEN COW-GIRLS GET THE BLUES

the electric cowgirl CAPSULE WARDROBE

For desert drives and Airstream adventures

Faded T-shirts sprinkled with sequins

Laid-back varsity sweaters

Vintage floral house dresses

For honky-tonks and neon nights

Plush faux-fur coats

Deep-V dresses in unconventional prints

Vintage ruffles and layered slip dresses

Footwear and accessories

Wear-with-everything backpacks

Round and cat-eye sunglasses

Beaded drop earrings

Hand-cut leather sandals

Braided bracelets

Hiking boots

Converse sneakers

Retro scarves and hair wraps

Cowboy hats

For ghost-town days

Pastel-hued organza pleats

Oversize surf sweatshirts and slouchy boyfriend jeans

Robe coats for cooler nights

the electric cowgirl
LOVES...

MOVIES: *Paris, Texas* (1984), *The Searchers* (1956), *Kings of the Road* (1976), *Urban Cowboy* (1980), *The Last Picture Show* (1971), *The Best Little Whorehouse in Texas* (1982). (What NOT to watch: *The Texas Chainsaw Massacre*, for obvious reasons.)

READS: *Even Cowgirls Get the Blues* (Tom Robbins), *No Country for Old Men* (Cormac McCarthy), *The Drifters* (Nathan Nix), *America Day by Day* (Simone de Beauvoir), *Last Stand: America's Virgin Lands* (Barbara Kingsolver)

BANDS: Gary Clark Jr., Shakey Graves, Stevie Ray Vaughan, Max Frost, T-Bone Walker, Janis Joplin, Willie Nelson, Asleep at the Wheel, ZZ Top, The Tontons, Black Joe Lewis, The Lone Bellow

TEXAS HIDEAWAY VIBES PLAYLIST:

▶ "Blue Eyes Crying in the Rain" (Willie Nelson)

▶ "When the Stars Go Blue" (Ryan Adams)

▶ "Dust to Dust" (The Civil Wars)

▶ "Oh Sing" (The Native Sibling)

▶ "Roll the Bones" (Shakey Graves)

▶ "Dark Was the Night, Cold Was the Ground" (Blind Willie Johnson)

▶ "Only the Lonely" (Roy Orbison)

▶ "Talk to Me" (Sunny & the Sunglows)

▶ "Side of the Road" (Lucinda Williams)

THE ROUTE

THE FREE-SPIRITED WANDERER: Our trip begins in Austin, which is easily accessible by plane from most parts of the country. Spend a day there, rent an SUV for the dirt roads, and head west—Marfa is a six-hour drive, and Terlingua is two hours south of it, along the border.

THE LONG WEEKENDER: Choose two destinations and plan to spend a day or two in each. You can start in Austin and head west to Marfa, or start closer in El Paso or Midland and take an evening sunset drive south to Marfa.

THE DAY(S) TRIPPER: Pick one spot and plan on spending your whole trip there. The easiest option would be Austin—a weekend in Marfa requires a flight and a lengthy drive in a rental car no matter what, and Terlingua is an even farther trek. Another option is traveling by train into Alpine, which is twenty-five miles from Marfa, and renting a car there.

AUSTIN, TX

Austin is warm and welcoming despite being one of the fastest growing cities in America. It's the kind of city that feels new every time you visit it, because the list of local hot spots changes every month: new venues, restaurants, juice bars, coffee-houses, boutiques. It's ever expanding.

On our trip, we'll stick to Austin classics. If you plan to spend a larger span of time here, be sure to seek out the local cafés and music halls and meet the craft-conscious makers, shop own-ers, and bartenders. These enthusiasts are usually eager to share ideas about their favorite new hangouts.

AUSTIN IN A DAY

HOTEL SAINT CECILIA: Secluded under six monumental oak trees, the Hotel Saint Cecilia has a decadent rock-'n'-roller-on-vacation vibe. The hotel design idea came from proprietor Liz Lambert's vision of her first guest as "Mick Jagger with a Bentley in the driveway." The online booking page is full of quotes from rock stars and writers to help you envision the vibe of each room. The lobby has a record collection to borrow from, and the mini bar is packed with local and global goods.

HOTEL SAN JOSÉ: Directly around the corner is Hotel San José, another fantastic place owned by the same hotel group. The San José offers an equally innovative experience at a much lower rate. If you're game for staying in a 1970s-style Ivy League dorm room, it's your place. Borrow a Polaroid camera or a vintage typewriter to document your trip. In the morning, get caffeinated at Jo's Coffee next door and snap a photo with the famous "I Love You So Much" mural.

WHAT TO WEAR IN AUSTIN

The Austin girl exudes a consummate cool. She rocks killer shades and bolo ties, sometimes with classic cowboy boots and sometimes with glitter-covered platforms. She knows every designer on the cusp of making it big—she's a sartorial hipster and an irreproachable trendsetter. For a lazy Austin afternoon, throw on your worn-in velvet, bell sleeves, and your favorite handmade leather accessories and head out into the sunshine.

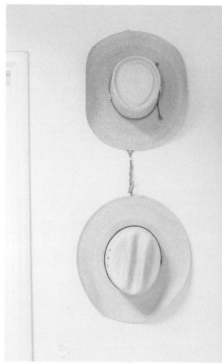

faux fur and cowgirl glam

BARTON SPRINGS POOL: In the early morning, grab
a bike (both hotels lend them out) and head to nearby Barton
Springs pool for a cool morning dip—there's no charge and no
crowd before 8 a.m. Play on the diving board or stretch out on
the lawn and make friends with the locals settling in for the day.
The Springs is open for night swims, too.

CASTLE HILL: Visit Castle Hill, an abandoned hotel com-
plex near downtown that's been converted to living art—it's
always being painted over, graffiti style. Join in, or people watch,
as skateboarders and BMXers whirl above the soda-pop-colored
ledges.

CAN'T-MISS AUSTIN

FOR THE FASHIONISTA: South Congress Avenue (SoCo) is lined with charming local shops and is on every style maven's list. Don't miss Archive for flawless designer finds from brands like Halston and Norma Kamali, ByGeorge for it-girl lines like Isabel Marant, and then take a look around Revival Cycles, a shop with a treasure trove of motorcycle gear and leather goods.

FOR THE VINTAGE LOVER: Shop the one-of-a-kind junk emporium Uncommon Objects for trinkets, visit Feathers Boutique for a mix of vintage leather and party dresses, and then travel over to End of an Ear Record Shop in the South First neighborhood where the famous "Greetings from Austin" postcard lives.

FOR THE PARTY GIRL: For a rowdy night out, take honky-tonk two-stepping lessons at The White Horse, catch a punk show or bands like Broods or Crystal Castles at Emo's, or play a round of Skee-Ball at Scoot Inn. There's never a shortage of riotously awesome things to do at night.

In the morning, stock up on snacks and water at the extensive Whole Foods (the chain was founded here), and be sure to get some cash out of the ATM, too—next, we're heading to lands where these conveniences will be no longer.

Austin to Marfa via 10 W to US-17 S (approx. 630 miles, 6.5 hours)

MARFA, TX

The sojourn to Marfa from Austin is an adventure in itself. The passage on I-10 West is uneventful, full of travelers passing from the eastern states to the far west. On our travels, we hit 17 South toward Balmorhea right around sundown. It's an itty-bitty town, no more than half a square mile from end to end, and, according to the map, the home of the last place to stop for a meal for the next sixty miles—Balmorhea Groceries, a small market with all the necessities and homemade burritos to go.

never leaving!

Marfa has gained a mythical status in recent years—if you haven't been, you've likely heard about it and the infamous Prada Marfa, which is actually thirty miles west in the ghost town Valentine. Marfa's place in the art world was cemented by artist Donald Judd's retreat there in the 1970s. Why he chose this space is obvious—there's no noise, visual or otherwise. An enchanted, psychedelic road show seemed to follow him there—hippies, surfers, and spirit seekers—a true convergence of cultures descended into Marfa.

Marfa is characterized by *dolce far niente*, or the sweetness of doing nothing. Bring your sketchbook or your guitar, and go out to gather inspiration from the artwork and the landscape all around.

When I told artist and designer friends that I was here, several shared stories of escaping to Marfa for their own extended artistic residencies. Wanderful girl Charlotte Fassler is one of those. Charlotte is the type of bohemian that takes sartorial dares with ease—Glossier pink cowboy hat? Hunter S. Thompson aviator shades? Double check. Charlotte worked as a photographer and resident illustrator for the widely influential Man Repeller blog and has photographed uber cool-girl brands Rachel Comey, Malone Souliers, and Collina Strada, to name a few. She's the ultimate Electric Cowgirl.

TWO DAYS IN MARFA

EL COSMICO: El Cosmico is an eighteen-acre vintage trailer park with teepees and yurts surrounding a communal cookhouse, hammocks, and soaking tubs. El Cosmico has a manifesto, or rather "mañanafesto": "If you have been to Marfa or places like it, you may have experienced Mañana. Mañana cannot generally be found in cities with more than one stoplight. Mañana doesn't care about email or normal hours of operation. Mañana recognizes that we can't all have everything we want at any given moment, like peaches in January or cell phone reception in West Texas. We are aware of a fascination with doing nothing that burns among us like a small rebellion inside our workweek souls."

THE FAXONIA: If you prefer to stay somewhere with an indoor bathroom (although there's something magical about showering under the stars), the Faxonia, named for the Faxon Yucca, is a converted old church that bills itself as "the place Johnny Cash would have stayed." Check out the highly curated Wrong Store at the Faxonia for hand-carved wood sculptures and unorthodox trinkets and gifts.

I HAVE ALWAYS LOVED THE DESERT. ONE SITS DOWN ON A DESERT SAND DUNE, SEES NOTHING, HEARS NOTHING. YET THROUGH THE SILENCE SOMETHING THROBS, AND GLEAMS . . . —ANTOINE DE SAINT-EXUPÉRY, THE LITTLE PRINCE

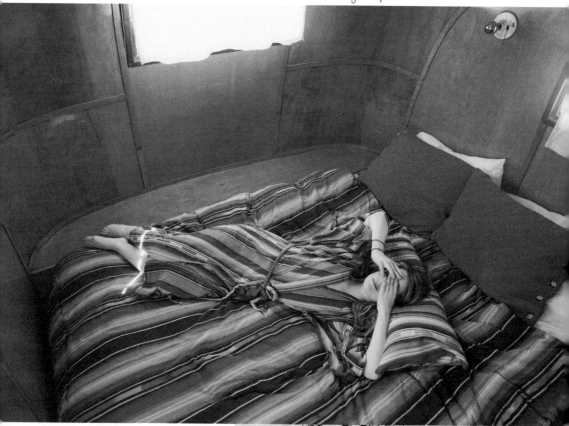

charlotte waking up in el cosmico

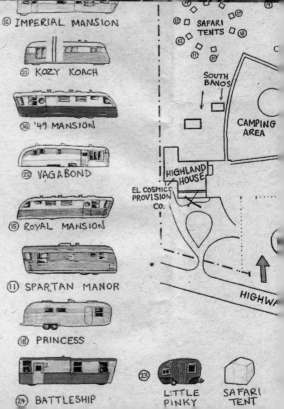

⑫ IMPERIAL MANSION

㉑ KOZY KOACH

⑯ '49 MANSION

㉒ VAGABOND

⑮ ROYAL MANSION

⑪ SPARTAN MANOR

⑱ PRINCESS

㉔ BATTLESHIP

㉓ LITTLE PINKY

SAFARI TENT

⑱ SAFARI TENTS

SOUTH BANOS

CAMPING AREA

HIGHLAND HOUSE

EL COSMICO PROVISION CO.

HIGHW

EL COSMICO   802 S. HIGHLAND AVE. MARFA, TX. 79843   TEL. (432)729-1950   www.elcosmico.com

Understanding that while yes, there are things to do in Marfa, keep in mind that most of your time will be spent practicing the art of slow living and, well, doing a lot of mañanafesto nothing. Here are a few places to take note of:

THE GET GO: Stock up on plenty of delicious goodies at this organic boutique grocer for a fireside meal or to restock your cooler.

THE GALLERIES: There are as many gas stations converted into galleries as there are actual gas stations. Even the food trucks and restaurants are mini art exhibits themselves. Spend the morning visiting the galleries and museums; they're full of mind-expanding, otherworldly exhibits.

EL COSMICO PROVISION CO.: Even if you don't lodge at El Cosmico, make sure you visit El Cosmico Provision Co., a rhapsody of adventurous goods, where you can stock up on sage, palo santo, leather moccasins, blankets, and all sorts of goodies that will make you the most popular girl at the late-night dinner campfire.

PRADA MARFA: This must-see fashion-meets-art mecca was built with biodegradable materials meant to slowly dissolve into the earth over time. The artists who created it intended it to serve as a surrealist commentary on Western materialism.

WHAT TO WEAR IN MARFA

The desert fashionista loves minimalism—channeling the sparseness of the whirling desert winds—and has an equal affection for extravagant celestial-inspired styles. In Marfa, art and fashion intermix. The Marfa style calls for layering peculiar and eclectic finds with furry jackets, tights, and scarves. The weather can swing by forty degrees in a day, so be sure to pack for the season.

little pinkie!

Miuccia Prada consulted on the project, providing bags and shoes from the 2005 collection, a version of which still sits in the window displays today. You'll likely find several other fashion lovers pulled over snapping Instagram shots upon arrival. Make the drive an hour before sunset for spectacular light.

MOONLIGHT GEMSTONES: On the way out to Prada Marfa, stop at Moonlight Gemstones, or as the locals call it, the Rock Shop (you can't miss it—rocks are piled all the way to the street). While there, I picked up a Texas agate, a moonstone, a tourmaline, and an amethyst. The proprietor, Paul, will even mount your stone into a brooch, pendant, or ring for you.

studying the cosmos

THE MARFA LIGHTS: Come nightfall, head out to Mitchell Flat with a blanket and a few beers to see if you can observe the Marfa Ghost Lights. In all honesty, you probably won't see anything paranormal, but the feeling of being alone in that desert oasis, lights or no lights, is worth it.

CAN'T-MISS MARFA

FOR THE ARTIST: Visit the Chinati Foundation to view the permanent installation of Donald Judd and a collection of up-and-coming contemporary artists; early risers should take the sunrise tour. Also on the list: Galleri Urbane, show-casing emerging artists; Ballroom Marfa, at the epicenter of town, offering avant-garde collaborations; and the modernist Eugene Binder gallery. Each is exceptionally distinct and worth the time.

FOR THE FASHIONISTA: Satiate your bohemian-style dreams at Freda for conceptual fashions, jewels, and house-wares from established and indie names. Check out Cobra Rock Boot Company for handmade Cuban-heeled boots.

FOR THE ROADSIDE CHEF: There's a long list of local food trucks, with Marfa Burrito, Food Shark, and Boyz 2 Men topping the charts, each with its own specialties. In town, stop by the modish Capri at the Thunderbird Hotel for killer cocktails in a gorgeous garden setting. The next morning, go to Mando's for a hangover fix, fast Wi-Fi, and a massive plate of whatever is on special.

Our next destination is one that requires serious grit—it's a commitment just to get there. Terlingua is best experienced by the traveler who's taking the Free-Spirited Wanderer trip. Keep in mind that the roadside inhabitants can be nefarious at times: Prickly trees, scorpions, and rattlesnakes aren't uncommon. On this drive, your phone will pick up cell towers in Mexico and tell you "Welcome Abroad." When traveling this close to the border, be prepared for border patrol stops.

Marfa to Terlingua, US-90 E to TX-118 S (approx. 110 miles, 2 hours)

WATCH WITH GLITTERING EYES THE WHOLE WORLD AROUND YOU BE-CAUSE THE GREATEST SECRETS ARE ALWAYS HIDDEN IN THE MOST UNLIKELY PLACES. THOSE WHO DON'T BELIEVE IN MAGIC WILL NEVER FIND IT.
—ROALD DAHL

TERLINGUA, TX

An off-the-grid border town, Terlingua is for the girl who embodies vagabond nonconformity. Like Marfa, the eclectic drifters and artists here have a sense of wild abandon and a pioneer spirit that's easy to settle into.

The places you'll visit in Terlingua are truly in the middle of nowhere—out here, commit to a few nights of solitude, scribbling poetry, and hanging by a late-night bonfire with your renegade crew—the night skies insist on conversations that turn to philosophy and astrology.

Make sure you travel in by daylight. If there was ever a time to pick up a paper map, it's now; GPS will send you careening down unmarked dirt roads. You have a few options for where to stay: Airstream glamping, rustic cabins, or a ghost-town inn. On our trip, we chose to stay at Tin Valley Retro Ranch in the middle of the Terlingua Creek badlands in a 1967 vintage Airstream, with an antique clawfoot tub and a donkey "watchdog" named Sampson. A little way away at the fork in the dirt road, you'll also find Terlingua Ranch Lodge, which offers horse corrals, a swimming pool, and the Bad Rabbit Cafe. Both options are under $100 a night.

Basically everyone here asked us the same two questions: "Where are you from?" and "How long are you staying?" The locals know that the bewitching charm of this place is intoxicating and can draw you in for more time than you intended.

TRUE ALCHEMY LIES IN THIS FORMULA: YOUR MEMORY AND YOUR SENSES ARE BUT THE NOURISHMENT OF YOUR CREATIVE IMPULSE.
—ARTHUR RIMBAUD

going riding!

TWO DAYS IN TERLINGUA

There are really only two things to do in Terlingua; however, the experience of those two things is powerful, which is why you'll need to take a little extra time. First, we'll hang out in the ghost town of Terlingua, and then we'll make a trip to Big Bend National Park.

TERLINGUA GHOST TOWN

One of Terlingua's highlights is the front porch of the Terlingua Trading Company—locals and tourists gather nightly to watch the sun slip below the pastel mountains here. The cast of characters you'll meet here is the main selling point. While we were there, we met a "doctor" offering "group therapy" and curing lost souls of "terminal unhappiness"—the prescription involved smiling and participating in the raucous good times happening on the porch.

The hotel, directly next door to the old trading post, is adorable and themed. It's touristy compared to Tin Valley or Terlingua Ranch; however, it's the center of the old trading post where the three dozen residents of the old town come to sip cold beers and lead sing-a-longs into the evening hours.

Take a walk down the hill to the Terlingua Cemetery. Modest filigree crosses, simple stonework, and small grottoes with handmade embellishments highlight this historic burial spot. Visit during a Día de los Muertos celebration to light candles and tell stories around the campfire with the locals.

way out in big bend

The stories we will tell . . . . Today we drove deep into a mud bog, too deep. We were stuck. No cell service, no paved road for twenty miles, if I was reading the map right, and all for a half an hour swim in the hot springs. Surely someone will come across our path. We waited. Hours and hours . . . nothing . . . . And then the coyotes started to howl . . . .
—A real-life journal entry from my visit to Terlingua

BIG BEND NATIONAL PARK

Big Bend National Park is massive. This isn't a day trip—the park is larger than the state of Rhode Island. It's remote, the setting of my journal entry opposite, and wildly diverse. The park encompasses the Chihuahuan Desert, the Rio Grande, and the Chisos Mountains. Before venturing into the park, load up on the National Park necessities: sunscreen, bug spray, bear spray, a traveling first aid kit, and jugs of water. Bring your bathing suit, a change of shoes, and layers of clothes (the hot days transition to cold nights).

There's so much to see—choose from desert, mountain, or river hikes, and pick one that fits your pace. We started with Santa Elena Canyon, a trail that crosses Terlingua Creek, ascends to

a vista overlooking the Rio Grande, and then journeys deep into the canyon. In the afternoon, take a drive into the Chisos Mountains. With an elevation of 7,832 feet, the Chisos Mountains house a relict forest of oaks, pines, junipers, madrones, and Arizona cypresses. At night, soak in the geothermic waters of the Big Bend Hot Springs. The water carries dissolved mineral salts reputed to have healing powers for the body and soul.

There's a lodge in the Chisos Mountains that is a good place to stay or dine and is worth stopping into at sunset for dinner and a slice of the daily pie special. Drive the one hundred miles of the park's paved roads for gorgeous vista views and incredibly photogenic geological diversity. There are miles of primitive dirt roads, too. The khaki-colored desert gives way to verdant forests of giant yuccas as you pass through old settlements and cemeteries. An important word of caution: It's critical to check with the rangers regarding road conditions before heading off the grid. (I learned this lesson the hard way and, despite quite a scare, got us out of that treacherous situation in one piece.)

Spending time out in these Texas deserts inspires a sort of romance with the things around you—romance with the lands, the travelers that came before, and those you're traveling with. It's a daring trip, made for the girl who isn't afraid of rugged roads and whiskey-town nights.

Returning home requires a lengthy drive—crank up the cowboy tunes and become one with the buzz of the road below.

WANDERFUL GIRL: AZA MARIA LUCIA ZIEGLER

Artist / Designer
Los Angeles, CA

AZA ZIEGLER is the designer of the cult clothing line Calle Del Mar, a favorite of *Nylon* magazine and the Knowles sisters. She travels to Marfa yearly to create new imagery for the Calle Del Mar collections. Aza's clothing has been described as attire that you have the best day of your life in. There are spoonfuls of star sequins sewn into her T-shirts—talk about good vibes!

In Aza's Bag:
A disposable camera and clothing from my line!

"I travel to get new experiences, explore new places, and to be inspired by new things. I was so curious about Marfa the first time I planned to go—what would I find in this colorful small town in the middle of nowhere? When I got there, I felt like I could stay and create art forever; everything is so aesthetically pleasing! While there, we stopped once to watch the moon and accidentally found ourselves on Texas private property. Uh oh! We had to backtrack one hundred miles in order to get back on the freeway. It was wild then, but it made for a good story once we made our way safely home."

CHAPTER

Five.

ROUTE 66

ROUTE 66 is comprised of tiny towns, one right after the other, on one of the longest stretches of road in America. At night, the neon signs that line the highway look like they're raising their glowing hands in the distance, welcoming you to the next little town. Romancing the 2,500 miles of road from Chicago to Los Angeles is no small feat. The Mother Road journeys through the heart of the United States, full of the country's most quintessential and kitschy roadside spots. We're starting at the midpoint of this incredible stretch: Amarillo, Texas. Amarillo is fifteen hours to Chicago in one direction, fifteen hours to Los Angeles in the other. We'll head west from Amarillo to New Mexico, the Land of Enchantment, through Arizona, and end under the luminous lights of Las Vegas.

morning in the grand canyon

disco time!

THE AMERICANA DREAMER

A FAN OF roadside drive-ins, records on a jukebox, and sundaes with cherries on top, the Route 66 girl is an Americana dreamer. She loves Betty Boop vintage styles, lace guipure dresses, distressed denim, leather boots, and her grandfather's hand-me-down Stetson hat. She makes fluorescent hues look like casual neutrals. She has an undying crush on Clint Eastwood circa *The Good, the Bad and the Ugly* (1966) and stays up way too late at night dreaming up tales with her best friends of what life would be like in an outlaw's paradise.

LISTEN TO THE MOTOR. LISTEN TO THE WHEELS. LISTEN WITH YOUR EARS AND WITH YOUR HANDS ON THE STEERING WHEEL; LISTEN WITH THE PALM OF YOUR HAND ON THE GEARSHIFT LEVER; LISTEN WITH YOUR FEET ON THE FLOOR BOARDS. LISTEN TO THE POUNDING OLD JALOPY WITH ALL YOUR SENSES.
—JOHN STEINBECK, THE GRAPES OF WRATH

the americana dreamer

CAPSULE WARDROBE

For diner hangouts and high-desert days

1970s-era prairie dresses

Easygoing vintage tops and maxi skirts

Worn-in T-shirts and denim layers

For neon nights

Silk slip dresses in vibrant and monochromatic hues

Beaded separates and leather bottoms

Off-the-shoulder and bell-sleeve silhouettes

Footwear and accessories

Aviators and cat-eye sunglasses

Bold novelty tote bags

Gemstone jewels

Patent-leather booties

Over-the-knee boots

Embellished wide-brim hats in leather or wool

Layers of metallic chains

Hand-tooled leather accessories

For ghost-town highways

Comfy loungewear in luxe fabrics

Oversize, slouchy sweaters and black skinny jeans

Sleeveless cotton shift dresses in a variety of prints

the americana
dreamer

LOVES...

MOVIES: *Easy Rider* (1969), *Bagdad Cafe* (1987), *Two-Lane Blacktop* (1971), *Thelma & Louise* (1991), *Bobbie Jo and the Outlaw* (1976), *Wild at Heart* (1990)

READS: *The Grapes of Wrath* (John Steinbeck), *Fear and Loathing in Las Vegas* (Hunter S. Thompson), *Freeways* (Lewis Davies), *American Nomad* (Frank Pickard), *Parallel Roads (Lost on Route 66)* (Dennis Higgins), *Hip to the Trip: A Cultural History of Route 66* (Peter Dedek)

BANDS: Journey, The Shirelles, Elvis, Asleep at the Wheel, ZZ Top, The Angels, Fleetwood Mac, Bruce Springsteen, Iron & Wine, Buddy Holly & the Crickets, Band of Horses

ROUTE
66 VIBES
PLAYLIST:

▶ "Long White Cadillac" (Dwight Yoakam)

▶ "Casino Queen" (Wilco)

▶ "Route 66" (The Rolling Stones)

▶ "Car Wheels on a Gravel Road" (Lucinda Williams)

▶ "Santa Fe" (Beirut)

▶ "No Particular Place to Go" (Chuck Berry)

▶ "Free Fallin'" (Tom Petty)

▶ "Lost Highway" (Hank Williams)

▶ "I Drove All Night" (Roy Orbison)

▶ "Take It Easy" (Eagles)

THE ROUTE

THE FREE-SPIRITED WANDERER: Through most of the western states, Route 66 follows Interstate 40 West, which runs about a thousand miles from Amarillo to Las Vegas. We'll be sticking to Route 66/I-40 for the most part, with a few detours. We'll start in Amarillo, travel along Route 66 to the Turquoise Trail Scenic Byway from Santa Fe to Albuquerque, and then head up to the South Rim or West Rim of the Grand Canyon before finishing the trip in Las Vegas, Nevada.

THE LONG WEEKENDER: Traveling by car from the east, choose one stretch of the Wanderer Route (Amarillo to Santa Fe, Santa Fe to the Grand Canyon, or the Grand Canyon to Las Vegas), and plan to spend a day or two in each destination.

THE DAY(S) TRIPPER: Choose one destination and plan to spend all of your time there. All of these destinations can be reached by a flight except for the Grand Canyon. Flying in to visit the Grand Canyon requires a road trip no matter where you come from—Phoenix Sky Harbor is three hours south, and Las Vegas is two-and-a-half to five hours west, depending on which entrance to the park you choose.

The Route 66 stretch through the western towns is a ghost highway—a terrain of high desert, saguaro cactus trees, and a landscape that often feels otherworldly.

AMARILLO, TX

Amarillo's Route 66 Historic District has nearly fifty family-owned and independent shops, including some rare and bizarre finds. Start this trip by wandering the thirteen blocks of this district on foot while taking in the sights of the Spanish Revival, Art Deco, and Art Moderne designs. Amarillo has some of the best vintage shops in the country, with remnants of prairie

treasures filling eccentric shops like Rag & Bone Antiques and Alley Katz Antique Emporium.

CADILLAC RANCH: Fifteen minutes west of the historic district is Cadillac Ranch, a public art installation created in 1974 by a crew of San Francisco hippies who called themselves "the Ant Farm." The installation features ten classic Cadillacs buried nose first in a sea of brown dirt. The cars have been spray-painted into a kaleidoscopic oblivion by art-anarchists for decades. Stop, join in, and give it your best Banksy—you're encouraged to!

PALO DURO CANYON: Travel thirty minutes south of Amarillo across the hazel-hued plains into the heart of the Texas Panhandle to Palo Duro Canyon, the second largest canyon in North America. The ideal way to experience the fourteen-thousand-acre state park is via horseback or hike. Stay over-night for less than $100 in a Civilian Conservation Corps cabin, a thirties-era stone hut that requires reservations made months in advance. Zigzag down into the basin and take in the park's famous hoodoo rock formations at sunset for a spectacular view of the multihued canyon walls.

About an hour after leaving the Amarillo area by car, you'll real-ize that you are, in fact, truly in the middle of nowhere. From here, there are two ways to approach the journey into New Mexico: Continue on Interstate 40 or exit at old Route 66 and make your way through the ghost town of Glenrio. As you approach the New Mexico border, the old road turns to gravel. If you're going to travel the gravel road, be sure you're in an SUV and traveling no faster than twenty-five miles per hour.

YOU SAID YOU AND ME WAS GONNA GET OUTTA TOWN AND FOR ONCE LET OUR HAIR DOWN. WELL, DAR-LIN', LOOK OUT, 'CAUSE MY HAIR IS COMING DOWN. —THELMA DICKINSON, THELMA & LOUISE

Once you've reached New Mexico, you will travel through the towns of Tucumcari and Santa Rosa on your way to Santa Fe—both are good stopping points. A ride through Tucumcari at night is a utopia of sparkling neon. If you're traveling through by day, visit the myriad of life-size murals paying ode to the ranchers, the cowboys, and the heyday of Route 66. Next is the tiny town of Santa Rosa, situated on the Pecos River. Stop for a swim at the Blue Hole, an artesian clear spring well, or grab a home-cooked meal in the downtown historic district.

40 W from Amarillo to Santa Rosa, New Mexico, 84 N to 25 W to Santa Fe (approx. 290 miles, 4 hours)

sun-bleached old west skulls

SANTA FE, NM

With an average of three hundred days of sunshine, there is no escaping the southwestern sun and that crystal clear sky of Santa Fe. The clouds look like they could be created by Pixar, something we found ourselves commenting on again and again during our travels.

Once you arrive in Santa Fe, head straight downtown to the Santa Fe Plaza, the art- and culture-saturated heart of the city. The city is one of the oldest state capitals, founded in 1610. Sink into the indigenous architecture in what is easily one of the country's most picturesque downtown areas. Santa Fe means "Holy Faith" in Spanish. It's a place people from all over the world visit to be captivated by the spirit of time-warped buildings and old churches at every turn, including the wondrous Loretto Chapel and the San Miguel Mission, America's oldest church. Just a short drive out of downtown you'll find hikes, trails, and a pristine wilderness in the Sangre de Cristo Mountains.

WHAT TO WEAR IN SANTA FE

The Santa Fe style? Classic cowboy or -girl: leather-tooled belts, turquoise rings, and sterling-silver charms. The Santa Fe girl loves lavender moonrise hues and sunset shades; she wears layers of denim and Southwestern prints. She carries a large-brim hat to shield her eyes from the midday sun and something warm for the evening, as the intense sunlight of day drops dramatically at night.

TWO DAYS IN SANTA FE

LA FONDA HOTEL: Stay in the famous and historic La Fonda on the Plaza. Considered one of the oldest hotels in America, La Fonda's history dates back more than four centuries, and its décor shows it—the place is steeped in Southwestern architecture, design, and artistic flair. In the summer, visit the Bell Tower, its rooftop bar, and take in the view of the expansive mountainscape just outside the city.

SILVER SADDLE MOTEL: If you prefer something a little less luxe, the Silver Saddle Motel is a roadside original complete with cowboy art and rooms named after icons of the West.

THE MARKETS: Start your day visiting the Plaza's Palace of the Governors. Shop the goods of more than 850 Native American artists including handmade textiles, leatherwork, carvings, ancient mirrors, and gemstones full of history. Santa Fe is home to the International Folk Art Market, the Sante Fe Indian Market, and the Traditional Spanish Market; if you're traveling during any of these you can spend half a day or more meandering among hundreds of vendors selling their intricately crafted works.

DEL CHARRO: In the afternoon, grab a Stuffed Green Chile Cheeseburger at this popular bar and grill. After a morning of gemstone hunting with Carrie Nash, a Santa Fe local, she sent us here to experience the Sante Fe staple, green chile, in a deliciously inventive way.

CROSS OF THE MARTYRS PARK: Cross of the Martyrs Park is the place to catch a spectacular Santa Fe sunset. Travel up Artist Road by car, or hike the wooden stairs to the hilltop on Paseo de Peralta, to experience one of the best westward-facing views anywhere.

SECRETO LOUNGE: Postsunset, visit this opulent cocktail bar in the historic Hotel St. Francis for a Smoked Sage Margarita—it has an earthy richness with a clean, fresh "garden-to-glass" flavor.

SUN-BLEACHED BONES WERE MOST WONDERFUL AGAINST THE BLUE—THAT BLUE THAT WILL ALWAYS BE THERE AS IT IS NOW AFTER ALL MAN'S DE-STRUCTION IS FINISHED. —GEORGIA O'KEEFFE

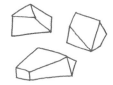

CAN'T-MISS SANTA FE

FOR THE COLLECTOR: Santa Maria Provisions has everything from specialty salt to French candles and Piñon incense. Their slogan is "eclectic provisions for a well-lived life," and it does not disappoint—while there, you're sure to find the perfect piece to add to your home.

FOR THE FASHIONISTA: Stock up on remarkably unique finds for your closet at Santa Fe Vintage Outpost. This adobe storefront houses Mexican peasant dresses, wool blankets, and reworked indigo Mali cloth alongside creations and jewelry from Zuni, Navajo, Hopi, and Santo Domingo tribes.

gemstone hunting in the plaza

FOR THE SPIRITUALIST: Ten Thousand Waves, a spa situated three-and-a-half miles up Ski Basin Road, is one of Santa Fe's hidden gems. Whether you're looking to take a soak in one of their public or private hot baths, get a massage, or have a great meal, it's a favorite for a relaxing girls' weekend.

FOR THE ART LOVER: The Georgia O'Keeffe Museum, an intimate space dedicated to the artist, includes an exhibit featuring painting supplies and still-life props arranged on a table in front of a window, an exact replica of what the artist saw when she painted.

"white bison" by kevin box

To reach Albuquerque, the next stop on Route 66, we'll take New Mexico State Road 14, the Turquoise Trail National Scenic Byway southbound.

On your way out of Santa Fe, make sure to stop for hearty home cooking from the San Marcos Café. The rural charm of the place extends to the Feed Store and grounds, where peacocks and baby chicks run freely.

Further along down the Turquoise Trail Scenic Byway stop at Origami in the Garden, a monumental outdoor sculpture exhibition created by sculptor Kevin Box. Motivated by the impermanence of paper, Kevin pioneered a new method of capturing its delicate detail with museum-quality metals. Each sculpture in the Origami in the Garden collection began with a single piece of paper, and it's quite a vision to tour the gardens and experience each one.

MADRID, NM

Midway down the trail is Madrid. In the early 1970s, bohemians repopulated the former coal-mining town, converting dilapidated Victorian homes and storefronts into gem shops and art galleries. Although it has a population of only about four hundred, visitors come to shop, experience the original tavern and soda fountain, the Old Coal Mine Museum, and the concerts and events that run throughout the summer months.

NM 14 S from Santa Fe to Albuquerque (approx. 72 miles, 1.5 hours)

ALBUQUERQUE, NM

Follow Route 66 through Albuquerque to get a view of the West Mesa volcanoes. On the way, travel westward through the vibrant Nob Hill area, where you'll find eclectic locally owned shops and boutiques.

Make a stop on Central Avenue to view the De Anza Motor Lodge, a burned-out motel on Route 66 that would have been torn down if it weren't for the priceless Native American artifacts it contains in its basement—seven twenty-foot-tall murals depicting the Zuni's sacred winter solstice ceremony. Pass the BioPark Botanic Garden, and continue on through historic Old Town and the downtown business district.

Finally, put on your brightest shade of red lipstick and stop into the 1950s-style, rockabilly 66 Diner. Have a Frito pie and the pink Cadillac shake prepared by real soda jerks at the soda fountain counter. Don't forget to bring some change for the vintage jukebox loaded with Elvis, Fats Domino, and Chuck Berry tunes.

40 W to 180 N, Albuquerque to the Grand Canyon, South Rim Entrance (approx. 410 miles, 5.5 hours)

THE GRAND CANYON, AZ

Fall into the rhythm of the road—the next destination west-ward bound on Route 66 is the Grand Canyon. Break up the drive with a stop in Gallup, New Mexico at El Rancho Hotel, "Home of the Movie Stars," a rustic treasure house full of Hollywood's Golden Age and Old West memorabilia.

About two hours out of Gallup, you'll arrive at the South Entrance of the Grand Canyon. Timing on road trips can be tricky, but be sure to arrive during daylight hours, because you'll want to catch all of the colors of the canyon during your first moments there. There are an abundance of things to do in the canyon—you could create scenic, adventure-packed itineraries for days.

Grandview Point is the perfect sunset-viewing location along the South Rim. Polychromatic buttes reach up from the canyon basin, and in the distance you'll see a sliver of the Colorado River far below. As the sun approaches the large peaks, find a spot to settle in and watch the glowing orange ball descend into the canyon. Tuck in for a peaceful night of solitude and a dizzyingly beautiful sunrise at one of the park's campgrounds or stay at a historic cabin at the park's Bright Angel Lodge.

When you're ready to get on your way, pass by the road to the South Rim and continue west on the old 66 mountain road to Kingman. From there, head north to the West Rim of the Grand Canyon to the cantilevered glass-bottomed skywalk, just 2.5 hours east of Las Vegas. The skywalk extends seventy feet over the edge of the canyon's rim, allowing visitors to look straight down to the canyon floor four thousand feet below.

US 93 N to Las Vegas (approx. 120 miles, 2.5 hours)

LAS VEGAS, NV

Technically speaking, Las Vegas isn't on Route 66. However, Las Vegas is an easy continuation of the route, and its glitzy neon night sky is one of the most iconic sights of modern times. It's a serious departure from the quiet of the ghost-town road—most people get sucked immediately into the glamorous casinos and the hotel pools. However, we'll be cruising the original downtown strip, Fremont Street, while swapping stories about mob-boss casino owners. This is a classic road trip ending and an opportunity to don your most decadent travel attire.

WHAT TO WEAR IN VEGAS

What to wear for a night out in Sin City? Skip the bodycon mini dress and instead opt for a silk slip dress and leather boots, a glamorous halter with stacked sandals, or statement sequins and velvet in a shimmering silhouette.

LAS VEGAS IN A DAY

THE LOCAL'S VEGAS: Start with coffee at Grouchy John's or brunch at Hash House a go go. Then, explore local favorite 11th Street Records for a vinyl listening party. An entertaining joint that may not be swarmed with tourists is Gold Spike, a former casino turned oversize backyard and music venue that features local bands.

all dolled up in indie designer krystal frame

THE NEON NIGHT EXPERIENCE: In the early evening, try out the hundreds of pinball machines and arcade games at the Pinball Hall of Fame or take in the jazz at the Dispensary Lounge. For an off-the-beaten-path night out, choose your favorite karaoke song and sign up to perform with the regulars at legendary Champagne's Cafe. If you're in the mood for dancing or trying your luck at a resort casino, go to El Cortez, downtown Las Vegas's first major resort, built in 1941.

CAN'T-MISS LAS VEGAS

FOR THE ART AFICIONADO: Visit the artists' studios of the 18b Arts District and experience James Turrell's *Akhob* exhibit at the Louis Vuitton store. Stay in the Artisan Hotel Boutique Hotel for reproductions of Cézannes and van Goghs, sinister sculptures, and Gothic décor.

FOR THE HISTORY BUFF: Take a night tour of Young Electric Sign Company's Neon Boneyard—wander along, learn the history of the city, and gain an entirely different perspective on Las Vegas.

FOR THE DIVE BAR LOVER: End the trip cozied up with the locals at any of the imaginative little taverns in the Fremont East Entertainment District. Favorites include Atomic Liquors, Don't Tell Mama, and Vanguard Lounge. Each has its own vibe, so bar hop to get in your last dose of neon.

After days on desert roads and nights under neon lights, crash in style as the sun comes up at an old-school Fremont Street hotel. Bid this Americana dreamer's trip good night.

OUR TRIP WAS DIFFERENT. IT WAS A CLASSIC AFFIRMATION OF EVERYTHING RIGHT AND TRUE AND DECENT IN THE NATIONAL CHARACTER. IT WAS A GROSS, PHYSICAL SALUTE TO THE FANTASTIC POSSIBILITIES OF LIFE IN THIS COUNTRY— BUT ONLY FOR THOSE WITH TRUE GRIT. AND WE WERE CHOCK FULL OF THAT. —HUNTER S. THOMPSON, FEAR AND LOATHING IN LAS VEGAS

WANDERFUL GIRL: ELIZA LUTZ

Artist / Musician
Santa Fe, NM

ELIZA GATHERS inspiration from the talent and diversity surrounding her in the local Santa Fe music scene. Her independent record label, Matron Records, was born from her passion for marketing, as well as her commitment to artist business education. As a dynamic and innovative creative agency, Matron is dedicated to collaborative storytelling through bringing together bands Eliza loves with businesses she supports.

In Eliza's Bag:
My labradorite necklace: it's the perfect protective talisman.

"Santa Fe is home to some of the most incredible and talented people I have ever met in all of my travels. It has a certain enchanting quality that magnetizes creatives from around the world who find their way to this small city in the high desert. They often never leave when they fall in love with Santa Fe's quirkiness and natural beauty. I am lucky to call this magical place my hometown and am passionate about building my life and my business here."

CHAPTER

Six.

WAY OUT WEST

THERE'S A MINIMALIST beauty to the southwest desert that makes it both meditative and alluring. Sand dunes, badlands, mountains, and valleys: There's a different type of stillness here. When you wake up with the first light, you can feel the tranquil energy emanating deeply from the sand below. This trip, a pilgrimage from White Sands to Joshua Tree, is about keeping things simple and summoning your vagabond spirit. These destinations have become a mecca for the fashion set: with colorful desert backdrops, spectacular rock formations, and the west coast light, there's unending photogenic inspiration. Spend your time tiptoeing over rocks, breathing in the fresh air, and reflecting on the outdoor solitude of the experience.

salvation mountain: a glorious temple of color

THE DESERT WANDRESS

THE DESERT WANDRESS is a creative free spirit and an introspective deep thinker. Her favorite way to relive her travels is by poring over the illustrations, photographs, and poetry she created with her road-tripping partners. She's memorized the constellations and sings lullabies to the stars. Inspired by rolling dunes nestled beneath the clouds from New Mexico to California, the desert wandress wears vintage gowns in colors pulled from her surroundings (her favorite color is high noon yellow). She climbs muted mountains and believes it's an enchanted world out there.

KNOW THAT YOU ARE NOT ALONE, AND IN THOSE HOURS WHEN YOU FEEL THAT YOU ARE, JUST KNOW THERE ARE OTHER PEOPLE OUT THERE SINGING THE SAME MELODIES OF WANDERLUST, CLIMBING OVER MOUNTAINS IN THE DARK, AND WAKING IN THE NIGHT TO STARE AT THE MOON, THINKING OF THIS LARGE WORLD AND DREAMING JUST LIKE YOU.
—APEX

the desert wandress

CAPSULE WARDROBE

For national park exploring

Printed crop tops and
graphic T-shirts

High-waisted denim and
cotton shorts

Utility vests or military-style
jackets

Hiking shoes and a backpack

**For rock 'n' roller
nights out**

Tapestry-printed
floor-length rompers

Folk-inspired separates

Batik skirts or dresses

Footwear and accessories

Oversize round sunglasses

Straw bolero hats

Wool safari hats

Fringe jackets

Distressed leather tote bags

Mini pouch bags

Moonstones and amethyst
stone jewels

Studded earrings and cuffs

Printed silk scarves

Suede knee-high boots

For oasis afternoons

Denim jumpers or overalls

1970s-era eyelet gowns

Breezy botanical-printed
maxis

the desert wandress

LOVES...

MOVIES: *The Darjeeling Limited* (2007), *Lo Sound Desert* (2015), *Joshua Tree, 1951: A Portrait of James Dean* (2012), *Young Guns* (1988), *Tiger Eyes* (2012), *There Will Be Blood* (2007), *Stones for Ibarra* (1988)

READS: *Wind, Sand and Stars* (Antoine de Saint-Exupéry), *Joshua Tree* (Rudy VanderLans), *A Field Guide to Getting Lost* (Rebecca Solnit), *Desert Solitaire* (Edward Abbey), *Going Back to Bisbee* (Richard Shelton), *Complete Astrology* (Alan Oken), *The Wild Girl* (Jim Fergus)

BANDS: U2, Queens of the Stone Age, Emmylou Harris, The Flying Burrito Brothers, The Rolling Stones, ZZ Top, Violent Femmes, Brian Eno, Sting, Best Coast, Wavves, Eagles of Death Metal, Kyuss

WAY OUT WEST VIBES PLAYLIST:

▶ "Arrested for Driving While Blind" (ZZ Top)

▶ "A Song for You" (Gram Parsons)

▶ "Romeo and Juliet" (Dire Straits)

▶ "Kashmir" (Led Zeppelin)

▶ "California Nights" (Best Coast)

▶ "Midnight at the Oasis" (Maria Muldaur)

▶ "Echo Canyon" (Sonic Youth)

▶ "High by the Beach" (Lana Del Ray)

▶ "The Passenger" (Iggy Pop)

▶ "Cherry Cola" (Eagles of Death Metal)

THE ROUTE

THE FREE-SPIRITED WANDERER: Fly into El Paso or Las Cruces and then travel by car to White Sands, New Mexico. From there, we'll head to Bisbee, Arizona, following I-10 West to 80 West. Continue on from Bibsee, then take 60 West to 62 West to get to Joshua Tree. The closest international airport to Joshua Tree is Palm Springs International, about forty-five minutes away.

THE LONG WEEKENDER: Both El Paso and Palm Springs have international airports, so it's easy to fly into one and spend a weekend nearby. If you choose the El Paso/White Sands leg, you can take a weekend trip over to Bisbee and back. If you choose Joshua Tree, use that as your home base and venture out on day trips to the Joshua Tree National Park and Salvation Mountain.

THE DAY(S) TRIPPER: Choose one destination and plan on spending all of your time there. You can fly into either the starting or end point of the Wanderer's trip for a day or two.

WHITE SANDS & LAS CRUCES, NM

We'll start this leg of the trip in Las Cruces. Less than an hour from the White Sands National Monument, this charmingly serene town is directly west of the Doña Ana Mountain range. A quick search on Airbnb will turn up the Nature Retreat. The retreat is a converted shipping container sitting on a beautiful five acres full of jackrabbits and all sorts of desert creatures. Unroll your yoga mat poolside and enjoy the location at the very edge of the desert, with a picture window facing directly toward the Organ Mountains—it's the perfect artistic hideaway. Wake up the next day with the sunrise and start your trek early into White Sands.

Taking a trip to White Sands, the largest gypsum desert in the world, is absolutely surreal. The bright white powder set against the azure blue sky is like nothing anywhere else in America— it's like something you'd find on a faraway planet, where fairy queens frolic in pastel gowns.

white sands bound!

WHAT TO WEAR
IN WHITE SANDS

The sand reflects the intense desert sun, so pack light-colored weightless fabrics to keep cool. The stark landscape is a vision—pack something magical to snap a few photos in and some cotton basics for sledding down the dunes. Wear leather sandals for dune hikes, adding an oversize wide-brim hat and your largest sunnies for protection from the elements. Temperatures drop dramatically after sunset, so pack lots of warmer layers for the cool night air.

White Sands is a destination to come prepared for—as you drive into 275 square miles of sand amid yucca and Cholla cactus plants, you'll encounter a sign: "No Water Available Beyond This Point." Be sure to pack several gallons of water in the car and keep sunscreen on hand. The sun is powerful, and the only shade comes from spaceship-like picnic shelters midway through the park. It's also smart to pack a compass—it's easy to get turned around quickly once you've hiked out even a little way into the dunes, and there may not be cell reception. The dunes are so soft you can tumble all the way down the highest one and feel as if you've rolled through a cloud. The gift shop rents sleds for this purpose (but you can bring your own!).

A few interesting tidbits about White Sands:

- The White Sands are an active dune field. They move from west to east as much as thirty feet every year, the winds leaving wave-like patterns in the sand.

- This is the Tulsarosa Basin, the site where a lake larger than the Great Lakes Erie and Ontario combined was located thirty thousand years ago. The fossilized tracks of mammoths, giant ancient camels, and saber-toothed cats have been found here.

White Sands is also an active missile-testing area—it's the location where the government detonated the world's first atomic bomb on July 16, 1945. Sometimes the park is closed for these tests.

This is a place so vast the only sound you'll hear, if any, is child-like laughter way out in the distance from the other visitors tumbling down the dunes on their sleds, making the vision of the vast stretches of empty dunes otherworldly. As we hiked farther into the dunes, the sounds floated away into nothing-ness. The silence was calming and mystical.

Time your trip to arrive in White Sands on the night of the full moon. From May to October, the park rangers lead a two-mile hike to meet the glow of the moon and the elusive creatures making the dunes their home. Registration for the hike is limited—it opens two weeks in advance, and the forty slots fill up quickly.

With a feeling of rejuvenation and newfound wonder, depart from White Sands and Las Cruces, venturing west to our next destination, Bisbee, Arizona.

Dip off I-10 at the junction where transcontinental Highway 80 continues on to Rodeo. There are few people and fewer businesses down highway 80, so stop in Road Forks to fuel up on gas, water, food, and supplies. For the next hour and a half, there will be more tumbleweeds, barrel cactus, and dust devils than humans or service stops.

Drive along the rust rock formations that jut into the sky above, crank up the radio, let the wind blow, and settle into that feeling of being but a speck of dust out on these glorious open roads. There are two small towns, Portal, Arizona, and Rodeo, New Mexico, about midway on the drive along 80, with no more than a few hundred residents peppered out in the desert hills. Make a pit stop in Rodeo at Desert Mountain Herbs to stock up on tinctures and sage bundles and at the Chiricahua Art Gallery for ceramics, jewelry, and wearable textiles made by local artisans.

Las Cruces to Bisbee, 10 W to 80 W (approx. 3 hours, 245 miles)

BISBEE, AZ

The initial views of the old copper mines are striking as you pull through Lowell into Bisbee on 80 West. Bisbee is a prime example of an Old West mountain town with a rugged natural beauty—streets twisting and lunging around hilly canyon views.

BISBEE IN A DAY

There's a beatnik bohemian vibe to this mining-town-turned-quirky-arts-colony. The historic Main Street, a narrow through-way, is brimming with inns, galleries, vintage shops, and boutiques. Above, clapboard cottages cling to the hillsides, as if they're peering down over the hippie community roaming about below.

Take a mental time out at the Shady Dell, a vintage trailer court with nine fully restored 1940s- and 1950s-era travel trailers for about $100 a night. Each trailer is completely decked out in period-appropriate décor. Our favorite was the thirty-three-foot 1951 Royal Mansion with its collection of 78-rpm records, leopard carpet, martini glasses, and diner-style kitchen.

WHAT TO WEAR
IN BISBEE

The Bisbee style is a hybrid of boho gallerista and mountain mystic. The Bisbee girl exudes a laid-back ease. By day, she wears denim separates, always aware of the desert elements. By night, she chooses garments rich in color and texture. When the weather is cooler, romantic prairie dresses can be paired with a turtleneck or a velvet scarf to cozy up for an evening out.

Shop up and down Main Street for vintage clothing and antiques—Finders Keepers and the Culture Pirate were our favorites. There, we picked up worn-in Levi's, a jewel-toned velvet blazer, and the perfect repurposed fur felt hat. Next, stop at Bisbee Soap & Sundry for handcrafted soaps, and then pick up a handwoven Panama hat at Óptimo Hatworks to shield yourself from the blazing western sun. For lunch, head to Screaming Banshee Pizza, and check the event calendar at the Central School Project cultural center. Drive just a few minutes down the road to tour Lowell, home to a street packed with classic cars. (It's not an exhibit. This is the real thing.)

In the evening, take a slow drive up the mountain on High Road, a skinny dirt road. Pull over often to take in the Lavender Pit below and the 360-degree panoramic views. Stay until the sun sets, then head back down to get dressed up for a visit to the Copper Queen Saloon. Sway into the night and have a bit of rowdy fun with the eclectic local crowd in a scene straight from an old Western.

Bisbee to Joshua Tree, 10 W (approx. 490 miles, 7 hours)

keiko blending in with the cholla cactus

WHAT TO WEAR IN JOSHUA TREE

The Joshua Tree girl channels the proper 1970s-era rocker. She dresses in glamorous vintage gowns or in leather, fringe, and concert tees. In Joshua Tree, she blooms. She's a delicate cactus flower who's stylish by nature, effortlessly mixing high-end designer finds with hand-me-down vintage beauties from her grandmother's closet.

JOSHUA TREE, CA

We'll end this spiritual journey deep in the Mojave Desert in the metaphysical mecca of Joshua Tree. There's a feeling of both connectedness and solitude that arises as you pass through the gnarled trees that give this area its name. It's no wonder that outlaw artists of the early 1970s went crazy for Joshua Tree's wide-open spaces and psychedelic enlightenment— time stands still out in this wild electroforce of a place. Painters, writers, poets, and musicians have been making the pilgrimage here for decades to surround themselves with monumental rock formations, Mojave yucca, juniper, and sage. John Lennon famously recorded "Imagine" and "Come Together" from *The Joshua Tree Tapes* here. Josh Homme, a Joshua Tree native and member of the bands Queens of the Stone Age and Eagles of Death Metal, created a musical collective at Rancho De La Luna called "The Desert Sessions." The sessions, dubbed "the longest-running mixtape in existence," have included upward of thirty artists, playing together for the love of music. There's a love story to enlightenment transcending this rare landscape.

TWO DAYS IN JOSHUA TREE

Drive into Joshua Tree with the top down, wind in your hair, and a sense of wonder floating out into the canyon air. There are so many interesting Airbnb options here, from tree houses to homestead cabins, each offering an extra-special experience and a shift in perspective. The Dome in the Desert, a 1980s-era geodesic dome stocked with books on palm reading and fortune telling, plus all sorts of knickknacks you'd want in your own home, is a favorite. Light up the palo santo and allow your inner creativity to be unhinged. The Dome in the Desert has served as a seasonal studio for fashion designers, painters, musicians, and photographers.

Once you've settled in, hit the Joshua Tree Open Air Certified Farmers' Market (if you arrive on a Saturday) and stock your home with fresh foods, coffee, and wine for the next couple of days. Then, head out to visit the Cholla Cactus Garden at the Joshua Tree National Park. As you approach, you'll notice that the flora begins to change dramatically from the higher elevation. Continue until you come to a peculiar area where the sun rays shine on the thousands of densely packed Cholla cactus plants.

THE SIERRA, A REGION SO QUIET AND PRISTINE THAT WE HAVE THE SENSE OF BEING THE FIRST HUMAN BEINGS EVER TO SET FOOT IN IT. WE FALL SILENT OURSELVES IN ITS MIDST, AS IF CONVERSATION IN A PLACE OF SUCH SOLITUDE WOULD BE LIKE TALKING IN CHURCH.
—JIM FERGUS

From there, drive about an hour and half south to the desolate Salton Sea to visit Salvation Mountain. Hyped in the 1950s as the French Riviera of the American West, the Salton Sea is a present-day resort ghost town where the water content is so salty it can't sustain life. The rainbow-colored Salvation Mountain, built with local adobe clay and painted with donated house paint, is a favorite destination for magazine editorial photo shoots, music videos, fashion-loving bloggers, and Instagram stars.

No trip to Joshua Tree is complete without a visit to Pappy & Harriet's Pioneer Palace. Standing on the site of an Old West Frontier Town movie set built by Hollywood investors including Gene Autry and Roy Rogers, this place is a roadside dream. Known for its mesquite barbecue and mac and cheese, Pappy & Harriet's offers raucous good times and intimate music shows with bands like Best Coast, Vampire Weekend, and the Pixies.

CAN'T-MISS JOSHUA TREE

FOR THE SPIRITUALIST: Schedule a visit to the Integratron for a chakra alignment and sound bath. The Integratron is an energy machine built on a geomagnetic vortex in Landers, California, twenty miles north of Joshua Tree. According to the creator, the wooden dome was built utilizing the design of Moses's Tabernacle, the writings of Nikola Tesla, and telepathic directions from extraterrestrials. According to the Website, "The structure is designed to be an electrostatic generator for the purpose of rejuvenation and time travel." The sound bath bowls are made of quartz whose "songs" are keyed to individual chakras. The sounds induce a deep, transformative meditation state that nurtures your energy field and relaxes your nervous system. You'll float out the door afterward.

FOR THE FASHIONISTA: Throughout Joshua Tree and the neighboring Yucca Valley are several boutiques and bohemian-chic vintage shops. Ricochet Vintage Wears (packed with groovy printed frocks), the End (curated by a Hollywood costume designer), Hoof & the Horn (full of Americana styles), Funky & Darn Near New (for leather, fringe, and cowboy boots), and Trailer Trash (stocked with handmade art, clothing, and music memorabilia) are all worth an afternoon of deep rack diving.

FOR THE CHIC DIY-ER: Visit in February during Desert & Denim, an alternative trade show featuring a gallery show, concert night, and campfire dinners. The show is for fashion brands creating handmade products that channel the rustic, homespun sensibility of Joshua Tree. Register in advance to attend workshops focused on natural dyeing, leather making, and perfume distillation.

FOR THE MUSIC LOVER: Integrate into Joshua Tree local life at the Joshua Tree Saloon for karaoke under a disco ball. Give the crowd your best Emmylou Harris and settle in for a night of cheap beer and deep conversations.

As you leave Joshua Tree, gaze up into the ethereal California sky, feel the heaviness of the humid air, and take off into the dreamscape, knowing you'll never forget the out-of-body experience this whole trip has been.

*MADNESS
PLANTS
MIRRORS IN
THE DESERT.
—FLORIANO
MARTINS*

WANDERFUL GIRL: ALLISTER ANN

Photographer / Director
Los Angeles, CA

THERE IS A captivating simplicity in Allister's work. Her subtle approach captures glimpses of intimate moments and situations. She finds beauty in the minimal. She's photographed artists such as Dolly Parton, Kenny Chesney, The Civil Wars, and Tegan and Sara, and she has worked with designers Billy Reid, Jeremy Scott, and Sophie Thallet, to name a few. When traveling, she focuses on packing light, making her an excellent road trip partner—she's forever ready for the next adventure at a moment's notice.

In Allister's Bag:

My camera, a poetry book, and journal, plus my passport, just in case the adventure continues elsewhere!

"Sunrises and sunsets have always been my place of inspiration, and some of my favorites have been in Joshua Tree. There is something very soft and quiet about being in the desert in silence and looking at the blend of colors beginning or ending a day. A favorite Joshua Tree discovery was the Cholla Cactus Garden. When you arrive, it's as if you are underwater and these cacti are seaweed from the ocean floor. The ombre colors and formations—there is really nothing like it! I thrive when I'm experiencing new places and photographing what I find there."

CHAPTER

Seven.

SOUTHERN SWAMPLANDS

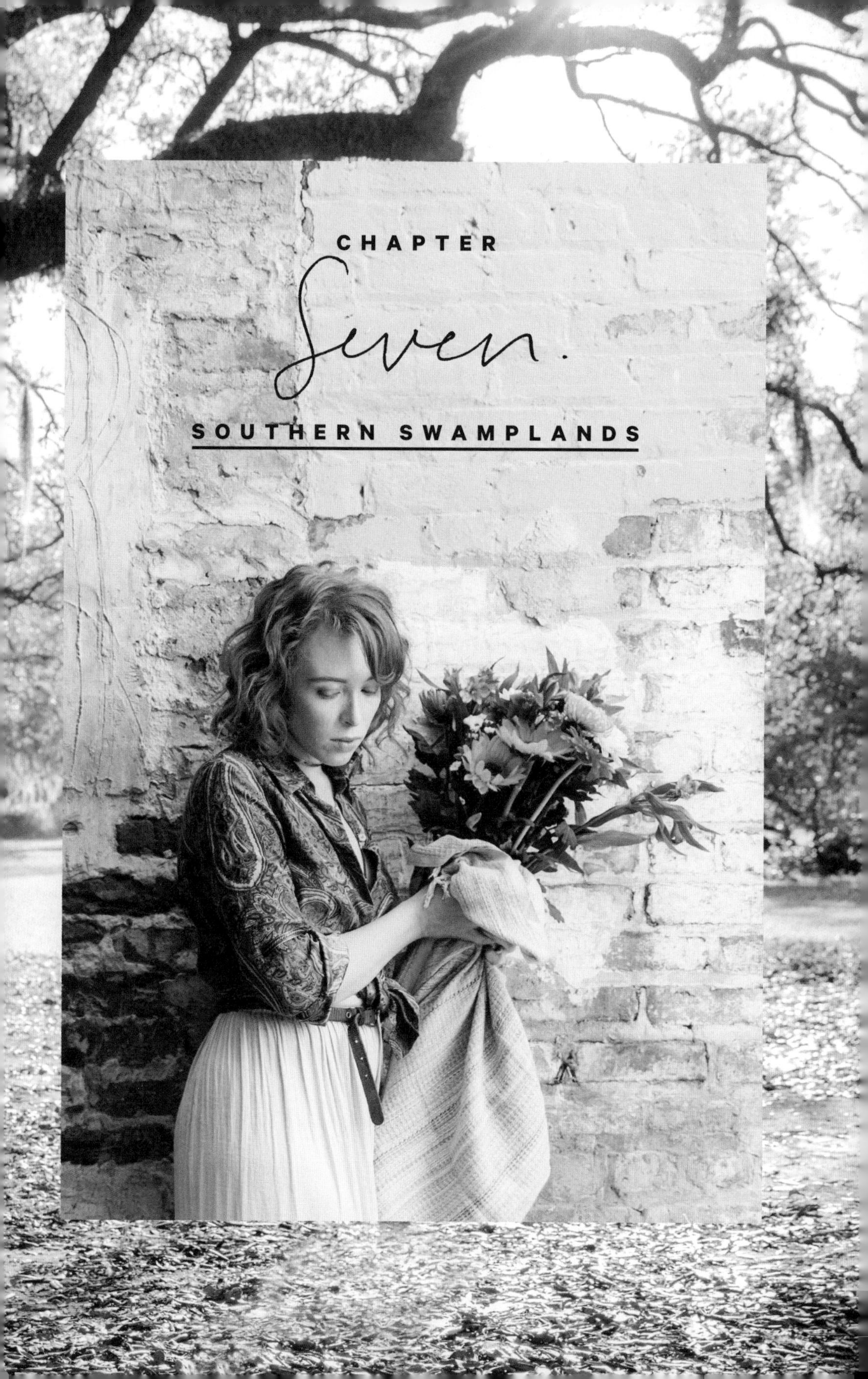

WE'LL START THIS adventure under the voodoo moon of Savannah, Georgia, then wander the sunshiney, daydreamy byways of the Florida panhandle, drive past the antebellum mansions and white sand beaches of southern Alabama and Mississippi, and then end our journey in New Orleans. Along the way, we'll meet everyone from budding bohemian artists and designers to longtime high-society residents and explore age-old hideaways in the swamplands. This route is a spirited trek where zydeco bands play under brooding night skies and a mélange of sounds and languages fill the streets. The architecture and people of Savannah and New Orleans exude a subtropical Gothic vibe that highlights the lives lived among the haunted houses, cemeteries, and highways.

weekend cruising

THE BOHEMIAN MOON CHILD

THE SOUTHERN SWAMPS cater to the girl who's confidently eclectic in style and spirit. She's a bohemian moon child who wears a dreamcatcher in her hair and whose everyday ensemble includes layers of vintage T-shirts, capes, caftans, charms, and beads. She's covered in stardust and glitter even in the daytime and dresses with a unique costume flair for every occasion.

WE DANCE EVEN IF THERE'S NO RADIO. WE DRINK AT FUNERALS. WE TALK TOO MUCH AND LAUGH TOO LOUD AND LIVE TOO LARGE AND, FRANKLY, WE'RE SUSPICIOUS OF OTHERS WHO DON'T.
—CHRIS ROSE

the bohemian moonchild CAPSULE WARDROBE

For exploring under the old oak trees

Breezy maxi styles in saturated color palettes

Gauzy, head-to-toe-white outfits

Comfy overalls, rolled up shorts, and soft T-shirts

For jazz clubs and brass-band-filled nights out

Exotic prints in relaxed fabrics

Colorful floral patterns and halter tops

1950s-inspired babydoll dresses

Footwear and accessories

Vintage sunnies

Layers of bright, chunky jewelry

Big buckled belts

Textured jackets

Leather crossbody bags or mini backpacks

Charm necklaces

Crystal and feather accents

Drop earrings

Stacked rings

Leather slides

Platform saddle shoes

Canvas sneakers

For traversing the low country

Vibrant crop tops and floral-printed midi skirts

Whimsical cotton voile separates

Mix and match flowy dresses and kimonos

the bohemian moonchild
LOVES...

MOVIES: *A Streetcar Named Desire* (1951), *Down by Law* (1986), *Interview with the Vampire* (1994), *The Curious Case of Benjamin Button* (2008), *Midnight in the Garden of Good and Evil* (1997), *Now and Then* (1995)

READS: *The Vampire Chronicles* (Anne Rice), *Midnight in the Garden of Good and Evil* (John Berendt), *Under a Hoodoo Moon: The Life of the Night Tripper* (Mac Rebennack), any of the plays of Tennessee Williams

BANDS: The Meters, Dr. John, GIVERS, Rebirth Brass Band, Etta James, Louis Armstrong, The Neville Brothers, Preservation Hall Jazz Band, Royal Teeth, Vagabond Swing, The Soul Rebels

THE SOUTHERN SWAMP-LANDS VIBES PLAYLIST:

▶ "Southern Nights" (Allen Toussaint)

▶ "Born on the Bayou" (Creedence Clearwater Revival)

▶ "I'll Make Time for You" (Kristin Diable)

▶ "Right Place Wrong Time" (Dr. John)

▶ "Lover on the Bayou" (The Byrds)

▶ "Sidestep Your Grave" (Andrew Duhon)

▶ "Feel Like Funkin' It Up" (Rebirth Brass Band)

▶ "Fancy" (Irma Thomas)

▶ "Summertime" (Sidney Bechet)

THE ROUTE

THE FREE-SPIRITED WANDERER: Start in Savannah, Georgia, where national and international flights arrive daily. Travel south on Coastal Highway, Route 17, toward Jekyll Island, Georgia. Continue south to Route 90 (the Old Spanish Trail Scenic Byway), and then drive along through coastal Alabama until you arrive in New Orleans.

THE LONG WEEKENDER: Spend two days each in Savannah and New Orleans. Between the two, take I-95 and then travel I-10 West for a quicker route. You can also just choose one location and spend your whole time diving deep into that city.

THE DAY(S) TRIPPER: Fly into New Orleans or Savannah—much can be covered in a day or two in either place.

SAVANNAH, GA

The essence of old meets brand-new swirls around Savannah and is present as much in the new wrought-iron elements as in the waving limbs of the ancient oaks. This city is home to an art and fashion scene of both the high-end and street-style varieties. From the Telfair Museums to shopSCAD, there's something to be uncovered no matter your aesthetic sensibility. It's a small city with a storied past; its Gothic architectural elements give it the appearance of being equally sweet and sinister, with each city square home to its own age-old saga.

The National Historic Landmark District's unusual layout—twenty-two squares dividing the city into wards—is the country's largest historic district and can be covered on foot, pedicab, carriage, or trolley. Each oak-shaded square, named for a historical figure with a monument honoring that figure in the center, forms its own mini park. Within, there are grand old

estates and verdant gardens canopied in Spanish Moss. The surroundings are cobblestone streets and alleyways.

shimmering moss and cypress trees

TWO DAYS IN SAVANNAH

THE THUNDERBIRD INN: First, drop your bags at this groovy motor inn at the edge of the historic district near Savannah College of Art and Design (SCAD). Reminiscent of the free-spirited era of roadside motels, it's a casual and fun-loving joint that brings the swinging 1960s to life. Each room is stocked with complimentary Moon Pies and RC Cola, plus a breakfast of Krispy Kreme donuts is served every morning.

BROUGHTON STREET SHOPPING DISTRICT: After settling in, wander up a few blocks to Broughton Street. Walk past the museums and theaters to discover eclectic shops like ZIA Boutique and KREWE, as well as contemporary designer spaces and kitschy junk shops tucked into the historic facades. Stop along the route for unique dining experiences at Alligator Soul or Circa 1875 (on the higher end) or grab a treat at the old-fashioned ice cream parlor, Leopold's. Another option is to detour a few blocks over to sample as many Southern dishes as possible at the cash-only Southern delight, Mrs. Wilkes' Dining Room.

STARLAND ART DISTRICT: On day two, visit the newly revitalized Starland neighborhood, a vanguard art district filled with tattoo parlors, handcrafted goods, floral shops, vintage boutiques, galleries, and vinyl record shops. The galleries in the area double as affordable artist studios and show spaces and have a mission of developing a sustainable creative economy in Savannah. You'll find it hard to leave without some special little creative find from one of the unique shops throughout.

CAN'T-MISS SAVANNAH

FOR THE FASHIONISTA: The two-story Paris Market and Brocante—part Francophile concept shop, part flea market ("brocante" means flea market in French)—is full of the world-traveling owner's quirky international discoveries. With the sensual sound of Juliette Gréco playing in the background, we scored a hand-carved feather chrysoprase dangle, made by a local Georgia artisan with a passion for found objects. Next, stop into the shared studio and storefront of local designer brands Mamie Ruth and M.Liz. Try on handmade wanderlust-inspired frocks and bohemian baubles among the vintage sofas and sewing table workstations.

ShopSCAD, a shop operated by the college, features clothing, accessories, photography, and paintings created by the students and alumni. With rising-star alums like indie designers Brooke Atwood and Hannah Goff, *Vogue* editors and big-name fashion designers (Marc Jacobs had a concept shop downtown) come to Savannah to see what the students and graduates are up to.

*SAVANNAH IS AMAZING WITH THE TOWN SQUARES AND THE HANGING MOSS AND THE FRENCH COLONIAL HOUSES. IT'S BRUTALLY ROMANTIC.
—DAVID MORRISSEY*

WHAT TO WEAR IN SAVANNAH

The Savannah girl's style is a mix of art-school librarian and tropical princess. She layers contemporary blazers and cardigans over vintage silk skirts and tops it off with kitten heels. She is warm and unpretentious, and her artistic know-how makes an appearance in the small details of her style—intricate chains, rare beads, and hand-carved pieces. She has a *je ne sais quoi* charm; she's the kind of girl who wouldn't think twice about showing up to a party with a deck of tarot cards tucked into her satchel.

In the Starland District, visit the Hidden Hand Society, an indie shop promoting local makers, Gypsy World, for well-priced vintage finds, and Urban Poppy, for one-of-a-kind flower crowns.

FOR THE ANTIQUARIAN: Take a tour of the Mercer Williams House Museum and revel in the opulent, and sometimes sinister, history. Restored by the antiques dealer memorialized in the now-classic book *Midnight in the Garden of Good and Evil* by John Berendt, the house was built in the 1860s for the great-grandfather of the songwriter Johnny Mercer. Mercer is famous for penning "Moon River" of the film *Breakfast at Tiffany's* (swoon!). You'll leave with serious interiors envy.

Just a step away is the treasure trove V & J Duncan Antique Maps, Prints & Books. Visit to pick up an autographed copy of

THIS PLACE IS FANTASTIC. IT'S LIKE GONE WITH THE WIND *ON MESCALINE.* —JOHN KELSO

Berendt's book or a map of the southern swampland region and have your mind blown by the incredibly rare antique maps meticulously cataloged by city, region, and year, dating back to the 1800s.

FOR THE BOOK LOVER: Pick up a copy of *Mystery and Manners,* by Georgia native Flannery O'Connor, and spend an hour or two in the reading garden at the Book Lady Bookstore. The forty-year-old shop offers rare and out-of-print books, as well as new titles.

When it's time to depart, pack up your indie designer finds and your leftover Moon Pies from the Thunderbird and head south.

17 S or 95 S to 10 W or 90 W to New Orleans (approx. 650 miles, 9 hours)

NEW ORLEANS, LA

I'll preface this conversation about New Orleans with a disclaimer: New Orleans is my home, and I've filled pages upon pages with recommendations of how to spend time here. And while much of the world's knowledge of the city, built on three hundred years of blended French, Spanish, African, and Caribbean influence, may be overshadowed by the biggest party on earth or that epic natural disaster, New Orleanians have always known their city holds a much deeper magic.

When I visited New Orleans for the first time in the one-hundred-degree temperatures of a July summer day, I was struck immediately by two things: First, there's the heat. It's sweltering but somehow, to me, comforting. There was a breeze coming off the river, and my skin glistened the second I stepped outside.

Second, music wafts into the streets at any given hour of the day. This isn't just a Bourbon Street phenomenon; in fact, the best music in the city—string instruments coupled with brass and a mélange of sounds—is typically tucked away in side-street venues. New Orleans's culture is rooted in music. There are musicians who perform in high-end concert halls and theaters and musicians who define themselves as "street entrepreneurs." It's a city where artistic survival and success is an integral part of the community. The city's icons have led movements like jazz and civil rights and inspired fashions copied by the rest of the world—festival fashion, flapper style, and seersucker's dapper dandies.

While the cuisine is what the city is often celebrated for (with great reason), following the French tradition of grandiose department stores and art galleries, New Orleans is a shopping destination and a mecca for Southern art. The retail stores stock the finest fabrics, employ tailors and milliners at the top of their trade, and offer custom exotic perfumes. The two gallery districts on Royal Street and Julia Street are lined with fine, contemporary, neo-street, and classical works, as well.

In a few days you can see so much—most things are biking distance (and you can rent bikes all over the city) or a streetcar ride away. Visiting during Mardi Gras in February is a remarkable, absolutely wild experience—something everyone should experience at least once. However, immersing yourself in the fashion and style of this vibrant city is fantastic any time of year.

TWO DAYS IN NEW ORLEANS

If you've got a couple of days to explore this dazzling city, it's best to pick a neighborhood or two and focus your time there.

Stay in the Catahoula Boutique Hotel, a restored creole townhouse on a side street away from the hustle of the Central Business District or the Old No. 77 Hotel & Chandlery, full of local artists' works and vintage charm—it's a renovated port warehouse just a few steps from the French Quarter. There's also the Ace, a local hangout of sorts. In the summer you can't beat the Ace rooftop pool!

THE FRENCH QUARTER: Since the founding of the city, the French Quarter has been the hub. Outside of the party vibe, people are drawn to the French Quarter for its Old World charm and French and Spanish architecture.

On the southern end of the neighborhood, the French Market, a two-hundred-plus-year-old market, includes stalls packed with tourist gifts, local art, and fresh produce. Vintage and flea market fans can visit David's Found Objects, SecondLine Arts and Antiques, and Le Garage, all on Decatur Street, steps from

the French Market. The residents of the neighborhood, ranging from high-society types to boho socialites, can often be seen surveying the action from their balconies and stoops.

THE MARIGNY AND BYWATER: Immediately downriver of the Quarter is the local's live music destination—the Marigny. Start on Frenchmen Street and work down to the Bywater, a thriving artist-friendly neighborhood home to a punk-style arts district along St. Claude Avenue. These two

neighborhoods are packed with some of the coolest hangs in the city, ranging from hipster dives to trendy design-forward spaces. Shop at Sterling Provisions for vintage housewares and Euclid Records for vinyl treasures including jazz favorites and obscure artists, and then visit the Bargain Center and the Pop Shop, neighboring junk shops tucked along Dauphine Street, for knickknacks and thrifty costume-style fashions. Local music clubs (it's like mini-Brooklyn, but shhh! no locals say that out loud) are perfect for an off-the-beaten-path night out. Some neighborhood favorites include:

- ☐ *Vaughan's Lounge:* A Bywater dive where local brass band stars play weekly
- ☐ *The Apple Barrel Bar* and *The Spotted Cat Music Club:* Live jazz every single night

beautiful french quarter balconies

WHAT TO WEAR IN NEW ORLEANS

The New Orleans girl has a devil-may-care attitude; she wears mixed-pattern and billowy handmade textiles in layers. Her look is representative of her laissez-faire lifestyle: She'll wear a vintage T-shirt with sequins and incorporate leftover Mardi Gras costumes and couture into her daily wardrobe. She loves jewels with a story: moonstones, amethysts, sun-charged crystals, oversize wooden beads, pendants, and charms.

☐ *Bacchanal Wine:* A let-your-hair-down joint that can be a daylong experience and includes a worldly menu, a backyard-style stage set-up, and a wine bar
☐ *Blue Nile* and *d.b.a.:* Groovy clubs for dancing along the "music district" of Frenchmen Street

The Marigny's hipster cred is long term—today, the Creole and Classic Revival cottages that stood abandoned have been restored. Historic banks, corner stores, and bakeries have been refurbished as homes and guesthouses, while revived riverfront warehouses offer artist studios and performance spaces.

THE GARDEN DISTRICT AND UPTOWN: The Garden District is considered one of the best-preserved collections of historic Greek Revival and Italianate mansions in the country, with lavish gardens and scenery to match. The streets bear the names of the nine muses of Greek mythology, and the neighborhood is home to Lafayette Cemetery No. 1, where Anne Rice once staged her own funeral, complete with horse-drawn hearse, in celebration of the release of one of her novels.

A PART OF NEW ORLEANS' BEAUTY IS THAT SHE IS A PLACE WHERE MANY PEOPLE, STIFLED ELSEWHERE, FEEL SAFE TO BE THEMSELVES. —QUO VADIS GEX BREAUX

Shop along Magazine Street, where you could spend a whole day boutique-ing.

THE TREMÉ: History is fully alive in the Tremé: The brass bands, second lines, jazz funerals, and Mardi Gras Indians parade through the streets as they always have, creating a pulsing experience. The style of the neighborhood, inspired by the early jazz days and the musicians who call it home, is the epitome of cool. Beloved jazz musician Kermit Ruffins has his own "speakeasy" in the neighborhood. It's a bit like an old-school supper club and in true-to-style fashion, Kermit's speakeasy has strong drinks, a quiet exterior, and no Website.

CAN'T-MISS NEW ORLEANS

FOR THE MUSIC LOVER: Begin your night at Preservation Hall in the French Quarter—it's worth the wait for the intimately authentic, acoustic performance by the Preservation Hall Jazz Band. Another French Quarter favorite is One Eyed Jacks, a swanked-out dive bedecked in velvet (even the art on the walls is velvet!). The roster constantly has local bands on the verge of making it big. As the night rolls on, catch a late-night funk show or brass band on the timeworn wooden floorboards of the swinging Frenchmen Street clubs.

FOR THE FASHIONISTA: Shop at the Vieux Carre's indie boutiques: Trashy Diva for pin-up styles and lingerie, Hemline for indie designers and it-girl finds, The Revival Outpost for hipster vintage styles, and United Apparel Liquidators for dramatically reduced prices on designer frocks. Hové Parfumeur is home to fragrance aestheticians and is known around the world for stocking the best in fine fragrances. Spend an afternoon on Magazine Street, making sure to hit Funky Monkey for eclectic vintage rompers, sunnies, and T-shirts, and Lili Vintage Boutique for high-society dresses and feminine, Southern silhouettes.

FOR THE GALLERISTA: Head over to the Michalopoulos Gallery to take in the dreamy interpretations of the city's architecture by the prolific artist James Michalopoulos. Then, walk the length of Royal Street and explore gallery after gallery interspersed with Parisian-style cafés and boutiques.

FOR THE NATURALIST: Venture over to City Park—a reminder of the city's wildness. The park, a 1,300-acre urban green space that, for perspective, is 50 percent larger than Central Park in New York City, includes a botanical garden, golf course, amusement park, and the New Orleans Museum of Art. Rent a boat to enjoy the pelicans and cranes along the Bayou. The park is also home to one of the hundreds of Louisiana festivals and to a local favorite taking place every year over Halloween weekend: the Voodoo Music + Arts Experience.

FOR THE COCKTAIL AFICIONADO: Stop by Cane & Table for Sunday brunch. Take a courtyard table if you can and try one of the award-winning rum cocktails served in a pineapple or ceramic tiki glass. Cure, a firehouse-turned-stylish-cocktail-lounge in the uptown Freret Street neighborhood, is great for a classic Sazerac, America's first cocktail. Lafitte's Blacksmith Shop Bar, on the southern end of Bourbon Street, is one of my favorite places to take first-time visitors—it's the oldest continuously operating bar in the country and was originally a pirate hideout. Make sure you order a Voodoo Daiquiri, which the locals order by asking for a "Purple."

After filling up on the colorful chaos of New Orleans, having your chart read by a voodoo high priestess, and sweating out sugary sweet drinks on the dance floors, point your car west once more to travel along the bridges and canals on the way to the airport.

*THROUGH PESTILENCE, HURRICANES, AND CONFLAGRATIONS, THE PEOPLE CONTINUED TO SING. THEY ARE SINGING TODAY. AN IRREPRESSIBLE JOIE DE VIVRE MAINTAINS THE UNBROKEN THREAD OF MUSIC THROUGH THE AIR.
—LURA ROBINSON*

WANDERFUL GIRL: REBECCA REBOUCHE

Artist
New Orleans, LA

REBECCA, a Southern-born-and-bred artist, paints wondrous things, both real and imagined. Her allegorical paintings of the natural world are coveted by devoted private collectors, as well as major brands such as Anthropologie (she's collaborated with the brand on numerous murals and housewares that sell out each season). Her wandering spirit makes her a worthy mentor of creative travelers everywhere. She taps into a timeless artistic student-of-the-world approach to painting her way around the globe. Rebecca gained recognition for a month-long solo journey project called "The Unlikely Naturalist," which pulled inspiration from Southern Gothic literature. She's also my favorite girl to attend a Mardi Gras parade with!

In Rebecca's Bag:

My pochade, a travel-size plein art paint box that fits in my backpack.

"There's a certain magic in following in the footsteps of great writers. This type of travel adds essential texture to creative work. I paint the flora and fauna of the South in a way that references the great naturalists and evokes themes in Southern Gothic literature. Traveling with this lens gives each destination a mysterious light and lyrical drama. You can't sit in a studio and paint the gritty stories of notorious characters. You have to get out in the mud, churches, swamps, dive bars, and backyards and live it. Along the way, your own experience becomes a part of the story. There's no replacement for seeing something firsthand."

CHAPTER

Eight.

ROCK 'N' ROLL HIGHWAY

ON THIS ROAD TRIP, we're heading to the magical places where legends are made: Music City and Gold Record Road. We'll be making stops where music makers and music lovers sometimes fly more than two thousand miles just to get their fix of the sound and the stage. These are the storied listening rooms and opulent theaters that launch new superstars into the stratosphere every day. From peeking behind the curtain at Nashville's famed theaters to hearing stories from the studios of The Shoals and the stages of Athens, Georgia, we'll discover a New South cool, where rustic meets modern.

behind the stage lights

here we go!

THE BACKSTAGE BEAUTY

THE ROCK 'N' ROLL highway girl is a backstage beauty. She plays an old guitar and carries it everywhere she goes. She lives by dirt-cheap rent and even cheaper beer. She throws the best house parties, knows the words to every Rolling Stones song, and she and all her friends are right on the brink of discovery. She's always the most laid-back, glamorous girl in the room in a thrifted 1960s-era gown, and dances right out of her platforms after hours. She travels with her best friends, going wherever the night takes them and falling into their motel beds only as the sun comes up.

IT'S ALL HAPPENING.
—PENNY LANE, ALMOST FAMOUS

the backstage beauty
CAPSULE WARDROBE

For sunny days on two-lane southern highways

Basic tanks, T-shirts, and super-frayed denim shorts or jeans

Oversize maxi dresses in luxe textures and fabrics

Dressed-up and embellished denim separates

For dancing in rock club dressing rooms

Chandelier dresses in flirty fabrics

A decadent 1960s-inspired high neck dress

Velvet wide-leg pants paired with a silk bow blouse

Footwear and accessories

Vintage and round sunnies

Wide-brim hats in a variety of colors and styles

Piles of beaded bracelets

Worn-in denim jackets

Leather mini backpacks

Layers of studded earrings

Oversize cocktail rings

Peep-toe platforms

Cowboy or combat boots

For thrifting, vintage, and vinyl record shopping

Fringe vests and jackets

Band T-shirts and flowy skirts

Monochromatic separates in a variety of textures

▶ "Tonight I'll
Be Staying Here
with You"
(Bob Dylan)

▶ "Making
Believe"
(Emmylou
Harris)

▶ "Tennessee
Jed" (Levon
Helm)

▶ "Wild Horses"
(The Rolling
Stones)

▶ "I'll Take You
There" (The
Staple Singers)

▶ "Songs That
She Sang in
the Shower"
(Jason Isbell)

▶ "Loves Me
Like a Rock"
(Paul Simon)

▶ "Sweethearts"
(Butch Walker)

▶ "Right Hand
on My Heart"
(The Whigs)

the backstage beauty

LOVES...

MOVIES: *Muscle Shoals* (2013), *Sound City* (2013), *The Thing Called Love* (1993), *Almost Famous* (2000), *Walk the Line* (2005), *Dazed and Confused* (1993), *Singles* (1992)

READS: *Cash* (Johnny Cash), *They Came to Nashville* (Marshall Chapman), *Life* (Keith Richards), *The Greatest Music Stories Never Told* (Rick Beyer), *Legends, Icons & Rebels: Music That Changed the World* (Robbie Robertson), *My Cross to Bear* (Gregg Allman)

BANDS: Alabama Shakes, Johnny Cash, The Whigs, The B-52s, R.E.M., The Black Keys, Karen Elson, Jack White, The Civil Wars, St. Paul and the Broken Bones, Kings of Leon, Chris Stapleton, Butch Walker

THE ROUTE

THE FREE-SPIRITED WANDERER: We'll begin our trip in Nashville and then travel to Florence and The Shoals via the "Gold Record Road," an easy two-hour drive. From there, we go east two hours to our last stop, the creative haven of Athens, Georgia, just a short jaunt from the big city lights of Atlanta.

THE LONG WEEKENDER: Plan to spend your time in either Nashville or Athens. From Nashville, Florence and The Shoals are an easy overnight getaway.

THE DAY(S) TRIPPER: Choose one destination and plan on spending all of your time there. Pro tip? Check the tour schedules for your favorite bands and pick a city based on where they'll be!

NASHVILLE, TN

In *The Thing Called Love*, I watched River Phoenix, Samantha Mathis, and Dermot Mulroney fall in love with each other, the sweet taste of stardom, and Nashville, all at once. Experiencing that film, I too fell in love with Nashville and the nomadic musician's life, and years later, I consider myself of the musically romanced variety. Nashville, like River's character, knows "there might be a song in that."

Once you arrive in Nashville, unpack your trunk of platforms and T-shirts at East Nashville's Urban Cowboy, a B&B guided by one fundamental principle: "Have a good time." Catering to the "artist or adventurer, designer or wanderer," Urban Cowboy is a Victorian mansion with eight unique suites, communal parlors, custom wallpapers, clawfoot tubs, and the hippest lean-to style backyard bar. Want something a little more private? Choose from the numerous craftsman-style bungalow Airbnbs in the neighborhood for a vibe that's eclectic and low-key.

If you prefer to be in the thick of the honky-tonks and the neon lights of Broadway, the Music City Loft is a good bet. Each room has a music association—there's an Elvis room, a Waylon room, and a room named for a Reba song, too. The location—half a block from the Ryman Auditorium, known as "The Mother Church of Country Music"—is a perfect spot for night wanderers planning to sip PBR while the cowboys sing into the wee hours of the night.

TWO DAYS IN NASHVILLE

BARISTA PARLOR: Get dressed in your best denim and start with artisanal coffee and cute-boy sightings at this trendy coffee shop. To place your order, step past the vintage motorcycles and peruse one of the hand-carved menus.

THIRD MAN RECORDS & NOVELTIES: Stop at Jack White's quirky record shop storefront attached to his recording studio. Shop for merch like T-shirts and turntables, reissued records, and Impossible Project photos. The Blue Room, Third Man's live performance space, is actually the only venue in the world where artists can record their performance direct-to-acetate, instantly producing a vinyl record.

WHAT TO WEAR IN NASHVILLE

Nashville girls are impeccably polished; they never miss a detail, from their glamorous hats to their hand-crafted jewels. They're masters of purposeful minimalism and homespun designer style. Whether it's retro rockabilly, vintage country boho, or feminine with a touch of hippie, the Nashville girl's style is skillfully approachable. What to wear for a night out in Nashville? Pull out your wide-legged pants and a button-up embroidered blouse, tie your hair up or let it flow, and dance your way into the night.

COOL STUFF WEIRD THINGS: Walk off your morning treats by heading down the road to this vintage and antique shop packed full of strange little odds and ends.

THE MURALS OF 12 SOUTH: Head over to check out the 12 South neighborhood, home of the famous "I Believe in Nashville" mural. (This neighborhood is more touristy than my typical recs, so if you're visiting on the weekend, be prepared for crowds.) Take photos with your besties at each of the murals including the striped walls of Reese Witherspoon's

Draper James boutique and the wildflower mural directly across the street.

PINEWOOD SOCIAL: Go bowling at Pinewood Social and marvel at the number of people snapping Instagram photos (join in!), and then head out to the pool and vintage Airstream food truck out back. There's a chance of a famous local musician sighting or two—it's a meeting place for the creative set.

FIVE POINTS: Venture into the heart of the Five Points neighborhood for the evening. You'll know you've found it when all the usual signs appear: bikes (fixed gear and vintage choppers), perfectly groomed beards, and gorgeous nuevo hippie girls in Gladys Tamez hats. Then, sweat out the day at the 5 Spot for a late-night 1980s dance party and grab a slice to soak up the High Life at the Five Points Pizza window, where every band that's on the tipping point of stardom is grabbing their 3 a.m. post-show pie.

THE CRYING WOLF: Commemorate the day by snapping two-toned photos in the booth at the moody Crying Wolf, one of the coolest hangouts in East Nashville.

CAN'T-MISS NASHVILLE

FOR THE MUSIC LOVER: Most visitors to Nashville come for the music, because there's truly so much to see and hear. Here are a few favorite spots:

- ☐ *Grimey's New & Preloved Music:* Go to catch touring bands hosting intimate in-store shows before heading downstairs to the Basement, a small-venue rock club known for its free "New Faces" nights.
- ☐ *Robert's Western World:* If you're ready to spend the night two-stepping at a real-deal honky-tonk, head to Robert's Western World. Fried bologna sandwiches, dancing cowboys, and cheap beer make for a memorable night down on the Broadway strip.
- ☐ *Grand Ole Opry:* It was 1925 when across the AM airwaves a radio announcer introduced Uncle Jimmy Thompson as the first performer on a new show, *The WSM Barn Dance.* Now, almost a century later, "the show that made country music famous" continues to feature a broad spectrum of country styles nightly. Take the backstage tour and gaze into the mirrors where gals like Dolly Parton and Carrie Underwood get dressed before their shows.
- ☐ *Tootsie's Orchid Lounge:* Legend has it that at this world famous historic watering hole, Tootsie kept IOUs behind the counter for the hungry musicians. At the end of the year, the Grand Ole Opry guys would pay off the IOUs for the up-and-comers to make sure Tootsie stayed in business.
- ☐ *The Ryman Auditorium:* The Ryman Auditorium is the birthplace of the Grand Ole Opry. Not only have the famous feet of Elvis and Johnny Cash grooved on the stages of this stunning Gothic auditorium, but the acoustics make it one of the best places in the country to see live music.

FOR THE VINTAGE DEVOTEE: An entire week could be spent diving into the vintage shops of East Nashville. On the best-of list:

- ☐ *OPIUMVintage:* This shop is stocked with a vibrantly obscure collection of pieces, including Japanese vintage sourced by owner Laura Citron.
- ☐ *The Hip Zipper:* Great for well-priced denim and accessories.

OPIUM
VINTAGE

- *Star Struck Vintage:* Star struck has an enviable selection, including gorgeous winter coats for under $100.
- *Local Honey:* On-trend vintage, featuring hand-dyed pieces by Magness Collection.
- *High Class Hillbilly:* The place for authentic cowboy goodies.
- *Goodbuy Girls:* Located in the Idea Hatchery (a test kitchen shopping center for new brands) this shop is great for graphic T-shirts and loads of fringe.
- *Old Made Good (OMG):* Just north of the East Nashville neighborhood is this kitschy vintage shop with a glitter-covered floor and adorably charming handmade goods.
- *Savant Vintage:* Over in 12 South, find this favorite of *Vogue* magazine, photographers, rock stars, and stylists—Savant has an extensive collection of highly curated pieces. Be prepared to spend a little more for the tremendous quality of the jackets, dresses, ponchos, and hats.

FOR THE INDIE FASHIONISTA: Music City has experienced an influx of fashion industry types, making the

hip boutique options as rich as the vintage options in recent years. At East Nashville's Two Son, find brands like Ace & Jig, Objects Without Meaning, and Two Son's in-house eponymous line in a space designed and curated by two couples, including James Kicinski-McCoy, the creative voice behind the blog *Bleubird*, and Leigh Watson, one-half of the musical duo the Watson Twins.

In 12 South, stop in to gas-stations-turned-modern-shops: White's Mercantile, a general store packed with hip little finds (owned by music royalty Holly Williams), and Imogene & Willie, a spot for hand-stitched custom denim.

Nashville is home to a new generation of fashion designers, partly as a result of the Nashville Fashion Alliance. Favorites catering to the modern boho girl are Simon & Ruby, for wanderlust-inspired jewels, Bone Feather, for leather goods, Ona Rex, for luxurious fabrics and interesting shapes, Hey Wanderer, for hand-stitched and -dyed kimonos, and Jamie and the Jones, for wearable basics.

FOR THE HIPSTER FOODIE: Mas Tacos Por Favor originated in a 1970s Winnebago and now resides in a storefront curated by what was surely a roving band of hippies who'd recently scored big at the flea market. Mexican street food–inspired eats like horchata and the carnitas tacos are the main draw, and the tortilla soup is best in show. Late night, hit Mickey's Tavern, a great neighborhood dive bar marketing itself as having no DJs, no karaoke, and no trivia, just solid hangs. It's the kind of place where the jukebox can go from a Sade song to a Led Zeppelin song, and everyone can sing along.

When it's time to depart, throw on that vintage dress scored at Opium and the hat stolen from your new band boyfriend and watch the city fade into distance as you drive down the Gold Record Highway to The Shoals.

Nashville to The Shoals via US-31 to Natchez Trace Parkway (approx. 122 miles, 2 hours)

THERE'S UNCONDITIONAL LOVE THERE. YOU HEAR THAT PHRASE A LOT BUT IT'S REAL WITH ME AND HER. SHE LOVES ME IN SPITE OF EVERYTHING, IN SPITE OF MYSELF. WHEN IT GETS DARK AND EVERYBODY'S GONE HOME AND THE LIGHTS ARE TURNED OFF, IT'S JUST ME AND HER. —JOHNNY CASH

THE SHOALS, AL

The Shoals community in Birmingham, Alabama, has a rich musical history, including classic favorites like Bob Dylan, the Rolling Stones, Aretha Franklin, and the Dixie Chicks, and more recently Jason Isbell, The Civil Wars, The Black Keys, and Band of Horses—literally thousands of musicians have traveled the hundreds of miles to The Shoals to record here.

A DAY IN THE SHOALS

The Shoals have become a not-so-underground hotbed for style. Here are some local favorites to check out during your stay.

- ☐ *The School of Making:* Schedule a workshop at The School of Making at Alabama Chanin, where wardrobe essentials in organic cotton fabrics are being constructed in the studio daily. (And make sure to try the pimento cheese at The Factory café!)
- ☐ *Billy Reid:* Next stop is Billy Reid's downtown shop for quality goods with a down-home wash. Visit in August to experience the brand's annual Shindig event. The weekend includes warehouse sales and pop-up shops featuring designers like Pamela Love and art exhibitions set against

MUSCLE SHOALS CHANGED MY WHOLE APPROACH TO MUSIC. IT AFFECTED ANYONE WHO EVER HEARD THE MUSIC THAT CAME OUT OF THERE. AND THAT'S PRETTY MUCH EVERYONE IN THE WORLD.
—DAVID Z, MUSICIAN/ PRODUCER

WHAT TO WEAR IN THE SHOALS

Florence, a community within The Shoals, is a place of true authenticity—it's grass roots with a rock 'n' roll appeal. It's also home to CFDA award winners and friends Natalie Chanin, of Alabama Chanin, and Billy Reid. Now is the time to re-create the style of your favorite grandmother—housedresses hand-sewn with organic cottons and tulle, quilted textures, and embroidered details.

a weekend of Southern music from bands like Dawes, John Paul White, and Rayland Baxter.

☐ *Music Studio Tours:* Travel across the river for a studio tour at FAME Recording Studios or Muscle Shoals Sound Studios, where famous musicians wrote and recorded some of the most popular songs of the last decade.

☐ *Seven Springs Lodge:* About twenty minutes south of The Shoals you'll find the Seven Springs Lodge, home of the Rattlesnake Saloon. Here, you'll find a few cowboys settling in for an evening at the saloon bar with their horses tied to the hitching posts outside while others warm up their guitars. This is your opportunity to meet the most authentic of them and explore more than twenty thousand acres of trails via horseback. Stay in a Silo Bunkhouse for less than $100 a night before taking off for another round of big-city fun.

The Shoals to Athens via I-65 S to I-20 E (approx. 330 miles, 5 hours)

ATHENS, GA

The rock 'n' roll highway girl is her happiest behind the velvet curtain, under the glow of stage lights. Athens, a college town packing serious rock per capita and our final stop on this trip, was made for girls like her. Athens has long been associated with springboarding indie and rock 'n' roll artists: R.E.M., Widespread Panic, The B-52s, Dream So Real, Of Montreal, and Danger Mouse all spent their formative years on stages here.

resting up before the show

WHAT TO WEAR IN ATHENS

The local girls of Athens know how to dress the part of the rock star (and they know how to hang like one, too). For a night out, layer on a denim jacket decorated with patches, pins, and velvet detailing and throw on some sparkling gold glitter eyeliner. Streamline your style with a tattered old T-shirt, your skinniest black denim, and the Doc Martens you've had in your closet since your teenage days.

TWO DAYS IN ATHENS

We got the grand downtown tour from a few members of Athens-born, garage-rock band, the Whigs. The guys took us to their favorite joints: To dine, they suggested The National for leisurely, boozy brunch after a late show night and Seabear Oyster Bar for new takes on retro seafood classics sourced from sustainable purveyors. To shop, they turn to Atomic for piles of art and vintage and retro styles, including handmade pieces from local designers, and Agora Vintage for designer classics like Chanel, Louis Vuitton, and Hermés. Each of the guys was wearing a pair of shades scored there.

heading to the festival!

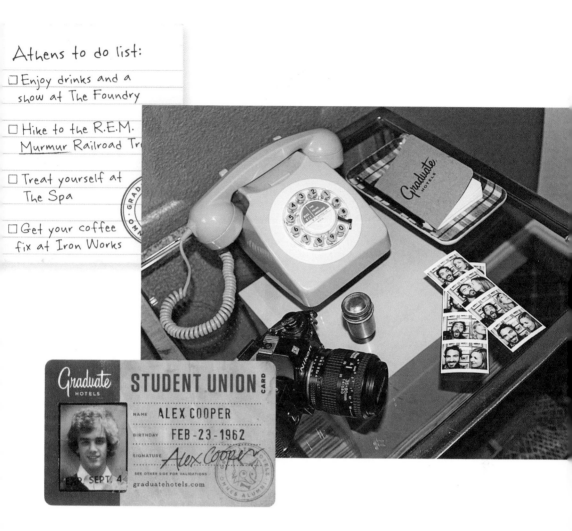

Athens to do list:

☐ Enjoy drinks and a show at The Foundry

☐ Hike to the R.E.M. Murmur Railroad Tr—

☐ Treat yourself at The Spa

☐ Get your coffee fix at Iron Works

Graduate HOTELS

STUDENT UNION CARD

NAME **ALEX COOPER**

BIRTHDAY **FEB-23-1962**

SIGNATURE *Alex Cooper*

SEE OTHER SIDE FOR VALIDATIONS
graduatehotels.com

EXP SEPT. 4

They also insisted we not leave without a visit to Wuxtry Records for 1970s first-press vinyl to take home as a souvenir from this adventure.

THE GRADUATE ATHENS: Pull into Athens and check into this playful boutique hotel that hosts live bands at its own music venue, the Foundry. Clever design details permeate this place—the rooms' traditional Southern décor is layered with University of Georgia collegiate flair and unique flea market finds for a nostalgia-inducing experience. Wondering about the formula on the chalkboards hung throughout the hotel? It's the chemical formula for a Southern classic, sweet tea, broken down by the university science department.

THE INDIE MARKETS AND FESTIVALS: Plan your Athens trip to coincide with one of Athens's indie markets, block parties, or music festivals. Wildwood Revival, Athfest, *Slingshot Festival*, Athens Popfest, and the Indie South Fair are each tailored to highlight what makes Athens unique.

THE MUSIC: Every night in Athens offers a packed music schedule. Check *Flagpole Magazine*, a local publication, to get a full rundown of nightly shows:

- *40 Watt Club:* Originating in a College Avenue loft apartment almost forty years ago, the 40 Watt is credited with pioneering the 1970s New Wave and punk scene.
- *Georgia Theatre:* Built as a YMCA in the late nineteenth century, the Theatre has hosted hundreds of artists in its time. Even if you don't catch a show, the rooftop restaurant has a fantastic downtown Athens view.
- *Caledonia Lounge:* An intimate, alternative venue featuring punk, noise-pop, grunge, and shoegaze-inspired rock from popular local bands and emerging artists from around the region. You can catch several bands in a night for under ten dollars.

As the trip comes to a close, pack up the set lists, wristbands, and all-access passes from night after night of music, turn up the playlist mixing your old and new favorite songs, and point the car back toward the highway to catch your flight home.

WANDERFUL GIRL: KRISTIN DIABLE

Singer / Songwriter
New Orleans, LA

KRISTIN HAS SPENT so much time out in the world as a touring musician and adventurer that she could be considered a true citizen of the world. She's the type of girl you'd find in a backwoods hippie commune headlining the nightly music show or on a grand festival stage inspiring people to hold hands and dance their tails off. She's a master of finding off-the-beaten-path places to perform: venues down old dusty roads and dimly lit dance halls where you don't quite know what good stuff is in store. She has a spirit that her fans connect with deeply, and a humor and hospitality about her that evokes an immediate sense of home. She finds the unknown to be magical and she writes songs reflecting that feeling.

In Kristin's Bag:

Essential oil spritzers: lavender and rose!

"I become brand new again every time I embark on a new road trip. Even places I've been before, there is always a new conversation, a new revelation, new insights to find along the way. There is a meditative quality to driving. The hum of the road, the reinforcement of the idea that you are, in fact, going somewhere. The external going keeps me aware of the internal going. This is a wonderful head space to find for writing tales of human experience."

CHAPTER

Nine.

THE GREAT NORTHWEST

GET READY TO HIKE the Rockies and dance across windswept prairies: The Great Northwest feeds the spirit where the Blackfoot once were king and the Buffalo roamed free. Trekking west on US 2, we'll wind along soaring mountaintops, rolling fields, and farms where small-town America is alive and well and then end our sojourn in Seattle, a seafarer's city that's impossibly cool. With giant cedar trees, craggy coastlines, and a lake created by ice-age glaciers, this route reminds us of what Lewis and Clark must have been searching for. We begin in beautifully rural Montana and travel west toward Seattle's modern gleam.

glacial lakes, crystal clear!

montana!

THE ECLECTIC EARTH MOTHER

THE GREAT NORTHWESTERN girl is an eclectic earth mother—she watches the wild horses run and finds herself equally untamed. Her heart is rooted in nature: fireside storytelling, brooding rainfall, and misty mountain summits. But don't let that fool you: She also loves a wild-child good time. She wears her trusty leather moto jacket over an old Henley with her denim tucked into her worn-in boots. At night, she ties her hair with twine, a golden feather tucked behind her ear as she twirls in a frayed hand-me-down gown and Avarca leather sandals. At home, her walls are lined with rustic artifacts collected during her travels. She feels freest when she leaves the cityscape behind and traverses out into the wide-open spaces.

FAERIES, COME TAKE ME OUT OF THIS DULL WORLD, FOR I WOULD RIDE WITH YOU UPON THE WIND, RUN ON THE TOP OF THE DISHEVELLED TIDE, AND DANCE UPON THE MOUNTAINS LIKE A FLAME.
—*W. B. YEATS*

the eclectic earth mother

CAPSULE WARDROBE

For National Park exploring

Distressed denim and lived-in thermal tops

Layers of destroyed T-shirts in subtle stripes and prints

For campfire afternoons and roadside photo ops

Luxe knits and versatile separates

Layers of multitextured fringe

Embroidered leather and relaxed-fit denim

Pendleton blankets to wrap up in

Footwear and accessories

Aviator shades and oversize round sunnies

Stetson cowboy hats

Denim and fringe-detailed accessories

Glossy bows and braided ponytail holders

Work boots for hikes through cityscapes, farms, and fields

Hiking boots and a backpack for mountain terrain

Studded bracelets and cuffs

Leather-tooled belts and accessories

For grunge-inspired Seattle days

Pink Floyd, Nirvana, and Pearl Jam band T-shirts

Oversize flannel and slashed denim

Black leather pants and a faux-fur coat

the eclectic
earth mother
LOVES...

MOVIES: *A River Runs Through It* (1992), *The Horse Whisperer* (1998), *Sweetgrass* (2009), *Powwow Highway* (1989), *Legends of the Fall* (1994), *The Twilight Saga* (2008, 2009, 2010, 2011, 2012)

READS: *Lakota Woman* (Mary Crow Dog), *In the Spirit of Crazy Horse* (Peter Matthiessen), *This House of Sky* (Ivan Doig), *Ceremony for the Choking Ghost* (Karen Finneyfrock), *Homebase* (Shawn Wong)

BANDS: Fleet Foxes, The Head and the Heart, Pedro the Lion, Death Cab for Cutie, Nirvana, Soundgarden, Mother Love Bone, Alice in Chains, Merle Haggard, The Highwaymen, Pearl Jam, Heart

GREAT NORTH-WEST VIBES PLAYLIST:

▶ "Pinesong" (A Fine Frenzy)

▶ "Little Wing" (Jimi Hendrix)

▶ "Quiet Houses" (Fleet Foxes)

▶ "No One's Gonna Love You" (Band of Horses)

▶ "Both Hands" (David Bazan)

▶ "Blue Rock Montana" (Willie Nelson)

▶ "Montana Song" (Hank Williams Jr.)

▶ "Lowdown Life" (Amos Lee)

▶ "Come as You Are" (Nirvana)

▶ "Rearviewmirror" (Pearl Jam)

THE ROUTE

FREE-SPIRITED WANDERER: Fly into Montana's Missoula International Airport, where half a dozen airlines offer daily flights. Then, head north on 93 to Flathead Lake, the largest natural lake in the west. Once there, choose your own adventure in one of the three lakeshore towns: Bigfork, Polson, or White Fish. Then, travel west on US 2 to finish your trip on the Pacific Northwest coast in Seattle.

FOR THE LONG WEEKENDER: Choose one destination on either end of the route, and plan on spending a few days exploring that area. On one end, you can fly into Missoula, spend a day there, and then travel up to Flathead to spend a few days in the towns surrounding the lake. (You can also fly directly to Glacier Park International, a small airport fifteen minutes north of the lake, serving about nine cities in Kalispell.) On the other end of the route, you can travel into Seattle and spend a few days exploring the farthest points of the Pacific Northwest.

FOR THE DAY(S) TRIPPER: Choose one destination and plan on spending all of your time there. A day trip or short weekend in our starting point of Missoula or ending point of Seattle is doable in that amount of time.

MISSOULA, MT

The views of Montana seen from the window seat while crossing into Missoula by plane are that of a nature lover's nirvana. On this trip, we'll rise early and end our days when the sun bids a late farewell each night. (It stays light late here—summer sunsets happen after 9 p.m.) This is an opportunity to detox from technology's itch and take in a simpler life, making choices based solely on the luxury of the land.

WHAT TO WEAR IN MISSOULA

The Montana girl loves classics with a love-child twist. She's timeless, like old photographs, and wears garments with a rock 'n' roll nostalgia. On the streets of Missoula, she blends in with the skaters in their tie-dye and the art girls in beads and fringe. Out on the range, she layers up in her boyfriend's old Henleys and flannels. She has a closet full of hats to choose from—both modern bohemian styles and a few passed down from her grandfather, too. She's the master of the lived-in look but always finds a way to add on delicately detailed accessories unique to her special style.

Missoula is a college town with a flourishing art scene. Its cultural heart is in the downtown area, a bustling central business district. Sidewalk cafés, craft microbreweries, galleries, boutiques, and youthful vibes abound.

MISSOULA IN A DAY

First, we'll drop our bags at the Shady Spruce Hostel. Joining the ranks of other stylized, high-end hostels, Shady Spruce is an iconic nineteenth-century Victorian home offering dorm-style accommodations and private suites. Share a room with your best girlfriends—the triple private rooms run about $100 a night.

Start the morning at one of Missoula's charming coffee cafés. Coffee shop culture originated in the Northwest, and each café offers something unique—it's easy to stay caffeinated here. On the list of good options: Zootown Brew, Catalyst Cafe & Espresso Bar, and Break Espresso. Also worth a visit is Butterfly Herbs, the oldest espresso bar in Missoula and a local favorite. Peruse the bulk teas and spices, botanicals, herbal tinctures, and tonics.

After fueling up, explore the shops and the sidewalks of downtown. In the heart of downtown, the Dark Room is possibly the best camera shop anywhere, offering a range of cameras, lenses, and accessories. For photography aficionados shooting 35mm film, the Dark Room will process your film within twenty-four hours, a big win for road trippers who want to develop as they go.

Then, sign up for an afternoon brewery tour. There are fifteen brewery options nearby, nine of which are in the downtown corridor. The breweries here are different: Imagine Nation Brewing Co. offers beer, of course, but also integrative community and personal transformation courses. Great Burn Brewing's name is a tribute to those who fought in America's largest forest fire. The passion for creating a variety of delicious brews is obvious, and the tours make for a great way to spend an afternoon.

CAN'T-MISS MISSOULA

FOR THE NATURALIST: Visit Brennan's Wave, an engineered whitewater rafting space on the Clark Fork River, which flows right through downtown Missoula. Grab a kayak or raft and hit the water, or hang on the rocks and enjoy the

I KNEW THEN THAT WHEN WE HAD CRESTED THAT FINAL TORTUOUS PASS IN THE ROCKS AND DROPPED DOWN INTO THIS VALLEY, WE HAD CROSSED A THRESHOLD INTO ANOTHER WORLD, A WORLD WITH ITS OWN SUN AND MOON.
—JIM FERGUS

spectacle. For a calmer ride, Zoo Town Surfers offers the "Downtown Float," a raft ride that will allow you to take in the sights of the city. As a bonus, it ends a short walk away from the "hip strip," a lively shopping and dining district on the west bank of the river.

FOR THE FASHIONISTA : Hippie girls will dig the shopping options: At Carlo's One Night Stand we picked up Levi's for under thirty dollars, vintage luggage tags, and lacy petticoats. Betty's Divine around the corner is another vintage star whose vibe is indie surfer girl meets classic American style. To complete your outfit, pick up a pair of locally handmade clogs from Bean-an-ti (Gaelic for "woman of the house") by designer Maren Lorenz, one of Betty's featured brands.

FOR THE MUSIC LOVER : Check out Rockin' Rudy's, a record rental shop opened in the 1980s. This self-proclaimed "hipster department store" is Missoula's hipster home base. Pet the fluffy cat lounging around and pick up concert tickets to one of the local shows. Dubbed Montana's cultural center, Missoula plays host to some of the most popular touring bands, so plan in advance to catch one of your favorites. Bands like My Morning Jacket, Lake Street Dive, Ryan Adams, Dr. Dog, and Grace Potter make regular visits to The Wilma—Missoula's premier music venue. Top Hat Lounge hosts free concerts and offers dirt-cheap tickets to indie acts like Hurray for the Riff Raff. In the summer, check out the music series for local acts at Snowbowl and Big Sky Brewing.

FOR THE HERBALIST : Visit Apothecary Esthetics—specializing in organic facials and botanical beauty treatments. Call ahead to reserve time in the sauna or schedule an in-depth herbal consultation or raindrop aromatherapy treatment.

Leaving Missoula, pack up your vintage scores, power down a double-shot latte, and hit the road—we're going off-gridding at Flathead Lake.

Missoula to Flathead Lake area, US-93 N (approx. 100 miles, 2 hours)

WHAT IS LIFE? IT IS THE FLASH OF A FIRE-FLY IN THE NIGHT. IT IS THE BREATH OF A BUFFALO IN THE WIN-TERTIME. IT IS THE LIT-TLE SHADOW WHICH RUNS ACROSS THE GRASS AND LOSES IT-SELF IN THE SUNSET.
—BLACK-FOOT

buffalo on
the plains

FLATHEAD LAKE, MT

Flathead Lake, tucked between the Kootenai and Flathead National Forests, is the largest natural lake in the western United States. With waters that are crystal blue and a minimal tourist scene, it's an empirically special place for wanderers to get away. Two scenic highways run parallel to the lake, allowing you to drive around the entire circumference if you wish. On the west side, travel Highway 93 (on the east it's Route 35), winding along the curving pebbled shorelines. Stop at trading posts for native jewelry and pick up huckleberry jams and cherry pies at roadside stands.

Worth the visit in itself, just east of the lake, is Glacier National Park. The main feature is the fifty-mile trek up the Going-to-the-Sun Road. The name is a native one, because the drive leading up is just that—a serpentine trail that seems to go directly to the sky. Climbing up from foggy forests on the west and snowy prairies on the east, plan to travel with four-wheel drive and be sure your emergency kit is stocked—Glacier National Park is nature on steroids. It's often June before the roads are plowed in full to travel what's often hours up the mountainside. If you'd prefer to leave the driving to the experts, take the stress-free and scenic shuttle tour from the Apgar Visitor Center.

There are several jaw-droppingly beautiful options for staying in Flathead Lake—it's hard to go wrong with scenery like this. Choose a B&B in any one of the quaint towns surrounding the lake. In the summer, be sure to book well in advance, as most are small and fill up quickly. Spend a day visiting the park and then choose your own evening adventure, settling into one of the following towns for a few nights before traveling to Seattle.

I WAS HEADED OUT DOWN A LONG BONE-WHITE ROAD, STRAIGHT AS A STRING AND SMOOTH AS GLASS AND GLITTERING AND WAVER-ING IN THE HEAT AND HUMMING UNDER THE TIRES LIKE A PLUCKED NERVE. ... THEN, AFTER A WHILE, THE SUN WAS IN MY EYES, FOR I WAS DRIVING WEST.
—ROBERT PENN WARREN

POLSON, MT

Peaceful and spirited set amid homespun natural beauty

Situated along the southern shore of Flathead Lake on the
Flathead Indian Reservation, Polson is a majestic mountain
town bordered on the south by the Mission Mountains and
surrounded by expansive cherry tree fields. Drive through the
National Bison Range on the route from Missoula to make a stop
at the Miracle of America Museum. Dubbed the Smithsonian of
the West, even the parking lot is an experience—you'll know
you're there when you spot the cherry sculpture dangling from
a crane. If you decide to stay in Polson, the place to be is Gaynor
Ranch. Fall asleep in a teepee by the Koi Waterfall for a spiritu-
ally grounding experience.

cherries are a montana specialty!

BIGFORK, MT
Sportsman chic mixed with an energetic art scene

Farther north you'll find Bigfork. Bigfork hugs the bay where
Swan River tumbles in. Bigfork's Old West downtown is adorably picturesque. Named one of the "100 Best Small Art Towns
in the Nation," there are galleries, boutiques, and delightful
cafés and restaurants. There are also innumerable options for
outdoor recreation; we visited during the Bigfork Whitewater
Festival, where hip, young outdoorsmen and outdoorswomen
converged on the town from everywhere to raft and camp all
along the banks, making for a fantastically fun party vibe. If it's
too cold for camping, there are plenty of cottage and condo
rentals nearby. Bridge Street Cottages, on the river's edge, is
a cozy rafting viewing spot and is walking distance to all the
local action.

WHITEFISH, MT
Warm and welcoming, full of roadside hospitality and charm

Thirty miles north of Bigfork, and thirty miles as the crow
flies south of the Canadian border, Whitefish is a popular ski
town during winter months. The people here are unbeliev-
ably friendly and laid-back. If you decide to stay here, there
are lodges and B&B options for regular crashing and the funky
little Whitefish Hostel for the budget nomad. The hostel café,
open to the public, has an organic juice bar and a full cooler
of healthy to-go goodies like coconut water, kombucha, quinoa
salad, and avocado pudding.

Central Avenue is the shopping center of Whitefish. While
there, pick up huckleberry hand cream (huckleberries are a
Montana favorite) at Crystal Winters and score a moto jacket
at leather retailer S. M. Bradford. S. M. Bradford also offers the
largest collection of Lucchese boots in the Northwest.

*Flathead Lake to Seattle via Hwy 2 W and US-90 (approx. 600
miles, 10 hours)*

SEATTLE, WA

We're going from rustic and charming to modern and booming as we make our way into the city. Seattle's a big city, with nearly 4 million people, and there are so many ways to enjoy it.

WHAT TO WEAR IN SEATTLE

The Seattle girl's style is down-to-earth—a blend of rustic bohemian rooted in old school rock 'n' roll. Seattle fashionistas have created a style movement all their own. It was home to the nineties grunge scene, and still Seattle girls rock Doc Martens and slashed denim with their tea dresses and bangs. It's also the land of Pendleton—everyone has at least a blanket or two in their closet. The Seattle girl rides a custom bike from Sweetpea, her basket full of farmers' market goods or painting supplies.

TWO DAYS IN SEATTLE

Seattle has two distinct vibes: woodsy and urban. For the naturalists, we'll explore the woodsy side by traversing trails nestled unsuspectingly throughout the city neighborhoods and then the National Parks, too. For the city dwellers, we'll spend our time exploring Seattle's quirky neighborhoods.

FOR THE OUTDOORS LOVER

Olympic National Park: Olympic National Park sprawls across several ecosystems, from the dramatically high peaks of the Olympic Mountains to lush rainforests below and wildly rugged coasts around the perimeter. The visitor center offers fantastic itineraries for both day visits and overnight stays. For a day visit, take the forty-five-minute drive from Port Angeles (where the visitor center is) to Hurricane Ridge, traveling from the lowlands to the tree line. Then, head to Lake Crescent and frolic along the shores of the glacially carved lake. Travel from Lake Crescent an hour farther west to get to Rialto Beach, where you can explore the beach amid driftwood and stones.

Mount Rainier National Park: Mount Rainier, an active volcano towering over the Cascade Range, is 14,410 feet in elevation. It's one the highest points in America, and one with a stunning presence. The best approach to Rainier is to decide on a base for exploration and head out from that point. If you want to see as much as possible, you'll need to do so via car. On our trip, we started early from the Longmire entrance to visit ancient forests surrounding the icy volcano's lower slopes and wildflower meadows. Head to Paradise next for bursts of brilliantly colored flora. Finish your journey by making the trek over to Sunrise for panoramic views.

FOR THE FASHION-LOVING URBAN EXPLORER
As we travel through each of the neighborhoods, there are a variety of boutiques and vintage treasures to dive into.

Ballard: With a relaxed and leisurely vibe, the Ballard neighborhood has transitioned from a Nordic seafaring village to a bustling hipster community. It's a blend of new families and youthful urbanites in Filson field coats and Zooey Deschanel hair bows.

Stay at Hotel Ballard, a renovated 1920s-era American-Scandinavian Bank with sixteen mid-century-style guest rooms. Before traveling to Seattle, we asked native Christine Cameron, personal stylist and editor of the popular blog *My Style Pill*, to steer us toward a few of her favorite things. First on her list: the French toast at Portage Bay Cafe and a visit to the touristy (but worth it) Ballard Locks to take photos and watch the vessels float by. After visiting the Locks, settle into a window booth at the Lockspot Cafe for fish 'n' chips and a craft beer.

For boutique and vintage shopping, Trove Vintage Boutique, filled with 1950s and 1960s finds, is packed with bright colors and delicately lovely fabrics. Lucky Vintage, another little gem, has a tightly edited selection of designer classics. At nightfall, head to the taxidermy den King's Hardware for a round of Skee-Ball and cocktails on the patio while alt-country tunes buzz on the jukebox.

Capitol Hill: The Capitol Hill neighborhood is closest to Seattle's famous tourist locales and offers an endless number of cool blocks to explore. The neighborhood is known for its

HE LIKED ITS SUBTLE, MUTED QUALITIES . . . VISTAS THAT SEEMED TO HAVE BEEN SKETCHED WITH A SUMI BRUSH DIPPED IN QUICK-SILVER AND GREEN TEA. —TOM ROBBINS

music—catch a hip-hop show at Chop Suey or New Wave pop at Neumos Crystal Ball Reading Room. Dig through the record bins at Sonic Boom and snap a photo of the Jimi Hendrix statue on Broadway near Pine. Shop at the eco-friendly Juniper for lines like Organic by John Patrick and Raleigh Denim, and meet one of the foster cats from the local shelter that call the shop floor their home.

christine, post-brunch,
waiting for boats to float by

The Ace Hotel in Capitol Hill is the original Ace location. Set in a former maritime workers' lodging building, it's a short walk to Pike Place Market, the Space Needle, and the lively waterfront. Rates are typically under $200 a night.

Fremont: The self-proclaimed "Center of the Universe," Fremont is a quirky little neighborhood on the north shore of the Lake Washington Ship Canal. Take a walk to see the troll under the Aurora Bridge and the dinosaur topiaries. Shop for local designer wares from Les Amis and Show Pony—two darling boutiques loved by the local fashion set. On the weekend, visit the vibrant Fremont Sunday Market, a European-style bazaar with goods ranging from deluxe junk to estate-sale treasures.

CAN'T-MISS SEATTLE

FOR THE ECO-FASHIONISTA: The heart of Seattle, with its bellowing buskers and fish-flinging merchants, is the bountiful Pike Place Market. It's a classic and quintessential way to spend a day and is as loved by the locals as it is the tourists. A few of our favorite market shops for the eco-fashion lover: Hands of the World, for fair-trade jewels; Conscious Wear, for eco-friendly goods; Earth Wind and Fire Boutique, for local designer wares; and 2nd Hand GALA, for well-priced vintage.

FOR THE MUSIC LOVER: Visit the Museum of Pop Culture housed in a building designed by Frank Gehry. This museum is home to one of the largest collections of music memorabilia in the world. Then, take in a show at The Crocodile, a storied venue that hosted Seattle's most famous early nineties grunge acts like Pearl Jam, Mudhoney, and Nirvana.

FOR THE SPIRITUALIST: Check out the Seattle Metaphysical Library, which has an extensive collection of books on magic, parapsychology, and extraterrestrial activity. It's hidden away in the basement of the Kress Building—look for the sandwich board on the sidewalk marking the entrance. Call to check for open hours before you go.

Return home from this journey feeling richer from the experience: As so many residents of these lands know, the Pacific Northwest is a feeling and a place that won't soon leave you.

WANDERFUL GIRL: SONORA MINDWERL

Artist / Traveler
Ashland, OR

SONORA GREW UP along the back roads of Oaxaca, Mexico, and spent her childhood visiting remote villages and traveling through mountains, jungles, and deserts. At the age of ten, her family piled in a van and road-tripped all the way to Oregon. With two seasoned traveler parents, the lifestyle soon became second nature to her, something she says is "as natural and essential as breathing." She paints snow-capped mountains and old-growth forests, creates illustrations of the muses and creatures that live amongst the Pacific Northwest trails, and takes photos of her adventures all while living out of her '97 RAV4.

In Sonora's Bag:
A water bottle, an extra pair of socks, and a pair of earrings to dress up!

"Being on the road is a steady stream of artistic inspiration. Going to new places every day and meeting new people means that I am constantly feeding my brain new images, ideas, and experiences. Surrounding myself with the beauty of nature calms my mind and allows me to focus my creativity, meeting new people introduces me to different ideologies and ways of life, and the inevitable problem-solving of everyday travel keeps me using new parts of my brain all the time. As an artist, the more I see, feel, and experience the better, and constantly traveling is by far the best way to get a steady supply of new experiences."

merci,

gracias,

thank
you...

To B E N for being my partner in life, in work, and on the road. What a life we get to live together.

To K I M P E R E L for guiding me from concept to outline to fruition. My wandress spirit truly came to life because of your dedication to the idea of this book.

To my editor C R I S T I N A G A R C E S, designer J E N N Y K R A E M E R, and the entire team at Abrams that worked so diligently to bring these travels to life, thank you for seeing and supporting my vision so clearly.

To A L L I S T E R and H U N T E R for being so generous with your time and talent. The photographs you both take inspire me daily.

To A M A N D A B J O R N for sharing the visuals you and Davey captured along the west coast. You've lent so much to the aesthetic of this book. You're truly the ultimate wanderful girl.

To my dear friend K E I K O G R O V E S, who traveled alongside me, thank you for sharing photos and encouragement always.

To K R Y S T A L B I C K, one of the most stylish women I know, thank you for sharing your incredible out-west adventures.

To C H R I S T I N E, R E B E C C A, K R I S T I N, S O N O R A, K A Y L Y N, E L I Z A, A Z A, C H A R, and each of the contributors in this book: All of you shared something so unique with your images and stories of your personal adventures. Thank you for being the muses to this story.

To L A U R E N for sharing a passion for my projects and guiding my thinking and ideas.

To A N G I E for encouraging me to take the first steps to bring this book to life.

To each of the wanderful girls (and a few boys, too): Meeting each of you (and taking your photos) on the road was an absolute treat. Thank you for trusting me!

To each of the brands and boutiques that shared garments with us, thank you for helping to illustrate "travel style"!

To my friends, family, and confidants, thank you for being present with me and with each other.

To the readers of my blog and my team, thank you forever for being in this with me! Your support over the years has given me immeasurable encouragement.

GLOSSARY OF PLACES

CHAPTER ONE: THE PACIFIC COAST HIGHWAY

Shopping

Shop Summer Camp
(805) 861-7109
1020 W Ojai Avenue
Ojai, CA 93023
shopsummercamp.com

Bart's Books
(805) 646-3755
302 W Matilija Street
Ojai, CA 93023
bartsbooksojai.com

Afterlife Boutique
(415) 796-2398
988 Valencia Street
San Francisco, CA
94110
afterlifeboutique.com

Wallflower Vintage Boutique
(415) 341-0314
1176 Valencia Street
San Francisco, CA
94110
shopwallflower.com

Mill Mercantile
(415) 401-8920
3751 24th Street
San Francisco, CA
94114
millmercantile.com

Everlane
2170 Folsom Street
San Francisco, CA
94110
everlane.com

Painted Bird
(415) 401-7027
1360 Valencia Street
San Francisco, CA
94110
shoppainted.com

Eats

Boccali's
(805) 646-6116
3277 E Ojai Avenue
Ojai, CA 93023
boccalis.com

Hip Vegan
(805) 646-1750
928 E Ojai Avenue
Ojai, CA 93023
hipvegancafe.com

Nepenthe
(831) 667-2345
48510 CA-1
Big Sur, CA 93920
nepenthebigsur.com

Fernwood Resort
(831) 667-2422
47200 CA-1
Big Sur, CA 93920
fernwoodbigsur.com

Big Sur Road House
(831) 667-2370
47080 CA-1
Big Sur, CA 93920
glenoaksbigsur.com/
big-sur-roadhouse

Big Sur Bakery
(831) 667-0520
47540 CA-1
Big Sur, CA 93920
bigsurbakery.com

Tartine
(415) 487-2600
600 Guerrero Street
San Francisco, CA
94110
tartinebakery.com

BiRite Creamery
(415) 626-5600
3692 18th Street
San Francisco, CA
94110
biritecreamery.com

City Lights Bookstore
(415) 362-8193
261 Columbus Avenue
San Francisco, CA
94133
citylights.com

Vesuvio Cafe
(415) 362-3370
255 Columbus Avenue
San Francisco, CA
94133
vesuvio.com

Caffe Trieste
(415) 982-2605
601 Vallejo Street
San Francisco, CA
94133
caffetrieste.com

Art

Ojai Valley Museum
(805) 640-1390
130 W Ojai Avenue
Ojai, CA 93023
ojaivalleymuseum.org

Landmarks

Meditation Mount
(805) 646-5508
10340 Reeves Road
Ojai, CA 93023
meditationmount.org

Point San Luis Lighthouse
1 Lighthouse Road
Avila Beach, CA 93424
sanluislighthouse.org

Hearst Castle
750 Hearst Castle Road
San Simeon, CA 93452
hearstcastle.org

Camatta Ranch
(805) 238-7324
9330 Camatta Creek Road
Santa Margarita, CA 93453
lazyarrowadventures.com

Henry Miller Memorial Library
(831) 667-2574
48603 CA-1
Big Sur, CA 93920
henrymiller.org

Big Sur Grange
(831) 667-2956
CA-1
Big Sur, CA 93920
bigsurgrange.org

Mission District Historic Murals
Mission Street
San Francisco, CA
94114

Mission Dolores Park
(415) 554-9521
19th St & Dolores Street
San Francisco, CA
94114
sfrecpark.org/
destination/
mission-dolores-park

Lodging

Ojai Rancho Inn
(805) 646-1434
615 Ojai Valley Trail
Ojai, CA 93023
ojairanchoinn.com

Madonna Inn
(805) 543-3000
100 Madonna Road
San Luis Obispo, CA
93405
madonnainn.com

Glen Oaks Big Sur
(831) 667-2105
47080 Highway 1
Big Sur, CA 93920
glenoaksbigsur.com

Nightlife/Music

Fremont Theatre
(805) 546-8600
1035 Monterey Street
San Luis Obispo, CA
93401
fremont.themovie
experience.com

Bimbo's 365 Club
(415) 474-0365
1025 Columbus Avenue
San Francisco, CA
94133
bimbos365club.com

The Chapel
(415) 551-5157
777 Valencia Street
San Francisco, CA 94110
thechapelsf.com

The Fillmore
(415) 346-6000
1805 Geary Boulevard
San Francisco, CA
94115
thefillmore.com

Spa/Wellness

Esalen Institute
(831) 667-3000
55000 CA-1
Big Sur, CA 93920
esalen.org

CHAPTER TWO: FLORIDA COASTIN'

Shopping

Lincoln Road Flea
Market
(305) 673-4991
800-1120 Lincoln Road
Miami Beach, FL 33139
lincolnroadmall.info

Alchemist
(305) 531-4653
1109 Lincoln Road
Miami Beach, FL 33139
alchemist.miami

BASE Superstore
Lincoln Road Mall
(305) 531-4982
927 Lincoln Rd #101
Miami Beach, FL 33139
baseworld.com

Books & Books
(305) 442-4408
2602 NW 5 Avenue
Miami, FL 33127
booksandbooks.com

Style Mafia
(786) 801-0319
2324 NW 5 Avenue
Miami, FL 33127
stylemafia.us

Malaquita Design
(786) 615-4917
2613 NW 2nd Avenue #13
Miami, FL 33127
malaquitadesign.com

Boho Hunter
(786) 558-4486
184 NW 27th Street
Miami, FL 33127
bohohunter.com

Sweat Records
(786) 693-9309
5505 NE 2nd Avenue
Miami, FL 33137
*sweatrecordsmiami.
com*

Ophelia Swimwear
(850) 213-0031
10343 E County Hwy
30A B120
Panama City Beach, FL
32413
opheliaswimwear.com

Alys Shoppe
(850) 213-5550
30 Mark Twain Lane
Alys Beach, FL 32461
*alysbeach.com/
amenities/alys-shoppe*

Perspicasity
(850) 231-5829
2236 E Co Hwy 30A
Santa Rosa Beach, FL
32459
perspicasityseaside.com

Central Square
Records
(850) 231-5669
89 Central Square, 2nd
Floor
Santa Rosa Beach, FL
32459
*centralsquarerecords.
com*

Monet Monet Maker's
Market
100 E County Highway
30A
Grayton Beach, FL
32459
30a.com/events

Grayton Beach Gypsea
(850) 231-4728
63 Hotz Avenue
Santa Rosa Beach, FL
32459
*graytonbeachgypsea.
com*

Eats

Jugofresh
(786) 472-2552
222 NW 26th Street
Miami, FL 33127
jugofresh.com

Panther Coffee
(305) 677-3952
2390 NW 2nd Avenue
Miami, FL 33127
panthercoffee.com

Charlie's Donut Truck
Somerset Street
Alys Beach, FL 32413
*alysbeach.com/dining/
charlies-donuts*

Fonville Press
(850) 213-5906
147 West La Garza
Lane
Panama City Beach, FL
32413
*alysbeach.com/dining/
fonville*

Modica Market
(850) 231-1214
109 Central Square
Santa Rosa Beach, FL
32459
*www.modicamarket.
com*

Bud & Alley's and Bud
& Alley's Pizza Bar
(850) 231-5900
E County Road 30 A
Santa Rosa Beach, FL
32459
budandalleys.com

Chiringo
(850) 534-4449
63 Hotz Avenue
Santa Rosa Beach, FL
32459
chiringograyton.com

Pandora's Steakhouse
Gulf Islands National
Seashore
(850) 244-8669
1226 Santa Rosa
Boulevard
Fort Walton Beach, FL
32548
*pandorassteakhouse.
com*

Landmarks

Grayton Beach Park
(850) 267-8300
357 Main Park Road
Santa Rosa Beach, FL
32459
*floridastateparks.org/
park/Grayton-Beach*

Lodging

Freehand
(305) 531-2727
2727 Indian Creek Drive
Miami Beach, FL 33140
freehandhotels.com

Mondrian South Beach
Hotel
(305) 514-1500
1100 West Avenue
Miami Beach, FL 33139
*morganshotelgroup.
com/mondrian/
mondrian-south-beach*

Delano Hotel
(305) 672-2000
1685 Collins Avenue
Miami Beach, FL 33139
*morganshotel-
group.com/delano/
delano-south-beach*

Pearl Hotel
(850) 588-2881
63 Main Street
Rosemary Beach, FL
32461
thepearlrb.com

Nightlife/Music

Gramps
(305) 699-2669
176 NW 24th Street
Miami, FL 33127
gramps.com

The Electric Pickle Co.
(305) 456-5613
2826 N Miami Avenue
Miami, FL 33127
*electricpicklemiami.
com*

Wood
(305) 748-2828
2531 NW 2nd Avenue
Miami, FL 33127
woodtavern.com

Bardot
(305) 576-5570
3456 N Miami Avenue
Miami, FL 33127
bardotmiami.com

Churchill's Pub
(305) 757-1807
5501 Northeast 2nd
Avenue
Miami, FL 33127
churchillspub.com

The Red Bar
(850) 231-1008
70 Hotz Avenue
Santa Rosa Beach, FL
32459
theredbar.com

Shopping

Good
(617) 722-9200
133 Charles Street
Boston, MA 02114
shopatgood.com

Crush Boutique
(617) 720-0010
131 Charles St # 1
Boston, MA 02114
*shopcrushboutique.
com*

December Thieves
(617) 375-7879
524 Harrison Avenue
Boston, MA 02118
decemberthieves.com

Coastal Jewelers
(207) 967-0100
28 Dock Square
Kennebunkport, ME
04046
coastaljewelers.com

Good Earth Pottery
Gallery
(207) 967-4160
7 Ocean Avenue
Kennebunkport, ME
04046
goodearthgallery.com

Portland General Store
43 York Street
Portland, ME 04101
*portlandgeneralstore.
com*

Find
(207) 699-4285
16 Free Street
Portland, ME 04101
foundatfind.com

Moody Lords
(207) 899-1149
566 Congress Street
Portland, ME 04101
*facebook.com/
Moody-Lords-
107106789346125*

Portland Architectural
Salvage
(207) 780-0634
131 Preble Street
Portland, ME 04101
portlandsalvage.com

Portland Flea-for-All
(207) 370-7570
585 Congress Street
Portland, ME 04101
portlandfleaforall.com

Eats

Liv's Shack
(860) 388-0246
26 Bridge Street
Old Saybrook, CT
06475
livsoysterbar.com

Island Creek Oyster Bar
Hotel Commonwealth
(617) 532-5300
500 Commonwealth
Avenue
Boston, MA 02215
islandcreekoysters.com

Ship's Cellar Pub
York Harbor Inn
(207) 363-5119
480 York Street
York, ME 03911
*yorkharborinn.com/
dining/ships-cellar-pub*

Tavern at Chapman
Cottage
(207) 363-5119
370 York Street
York Harbor, ME 03911
*yorkharborinn.com/
dining/tavern-
chapman-cottage*

Nunan's Lobster Hut
(207) 967-4362
9 Mills Road
Kennebunkport, ME
04046
nunanslobsterhut.com

Eventide Oyster Co.
(207) 774-8538
86 Middle Street
Portland, ME 04101
eventideoysterco.com

Landmarks

"Wedding Cake"
House
(207) 985-9333
105 Summer Street
Kennebunk, ME 04043

Maxwell's Farm
(207) 799-3383
527 Ocean House Road
Cape Elizabeth, ME
04107
maxwellsfarm.com

Portland Head Light
(207) 799-2661
1000 Shore Road
Cape Elizabeth, ME
04107
portlandheadlight.com

Portland Observatory
(207) 774-5561
138 Congress Street
Portland, ME 04101
*portlandlandmarks.org/
observatory*

Lodging

York Harbor Inn
(207) 363-5119
480 York Street
York, ME 03911
yorkharborinn.com

Captain Jefferds Inn
(207) 967-2311
5 Pearl Street
Kennebunkport, ME
04046
captainjefferdsinn.com

Inn by the Sea
(207) 799-3134
40 Bowery Beach Road
Cape Elizabeth, ME
04107
innbythesea.com

Shopping

Archive
(214) 546-0284
1708 S Congress
Avenue
Austin, TX 78704
archivevintage.com

ByGeorge
(512) 441-8600
1400 S Congress
Avenue
Austin, TX 78704
bygeorgeaustin.com

Revival Cycles
(512) 291-3377
5305 Bolm Road #1
Austin, TX 78721
revivalcycles.com

Uncommon Objects
(512) 442-4000
1512 S Congress Avenue
Austin, TX 78704
uncommonobjects.com

Feathers Boutique
(512) 912-9779
1700B S Congress
Avenue
Austin, TX 78704
*feathersboutique
vintage.com*

End of an Ear
(512) 462-6008
4304 Clawson Road
Austin, TX 78704
endofanear.com

**El Cosmico
Provision Co.**
(432) 729-1950
802 S Highland Avenue
Marfa, TX 79843
ecprovisionco.com

Moonlight Gemstones
(432) 729-4526
1220, 1001 W San
Antonio Street
Marfa, TX 79843
*moonlightgemstones.
com*

Freda
(432) 729-2000
207 S Highland Avenue
Marfa, TX 79843
shop-freda.com

**Cobra Rock Boot
Company**
(806) 549-0185
107 South Dean Street
Marfa, TX 79843
cobrarock.com

**Terlingua Trading
Company**
(432) 371-2234
100 Ivey Street
Terlingua, TX 79852
*terlinguatradingco.
homestead.com*

Eats

Jo's Coffee
(512) 469-9003
242 W 2nd Street
Austin, TX 78701
joscoffee.com

Balmorhea Groceries
(432) 375-2425
402 S Main Street
Balmorhea, TX 79718

The Get Go
(432) 729-3335
208 S Dean Street
Marfa, TX 79843
*mirthmarfa.com/
thegetgo*

Marfa Burrito
(325) 514-8675
104 E Waco Street
Marfa, TX 79843
*facebook.com/pages/
Marfa-Burrittos/
114897698569046*

Food Shark
(432) 207-2090
909 West San Antonio
Street / Highway 90
Marfa, TX 79843
foodsharkmarfa.com

Boyz 2 Men
(432) 729-7300
300 W San Antonio
Street
Marfa, TX 79843
*facebook.com/
boyz2menmarfa*

**Capri at the
Thunderbird**
Thunderbird Hotel
(432) 729-1984
601 W San Antonio
Street
Marfa, TX 79843
*thunderbirdmarfa.com/
capri*

**Mando's Restaurant
& Bar**
(432) 729-8170
1506 W San Antonio
Street
Marfa, TX 79843
*facebook.com/
MandosRestaurant
MarfaTX*

Art

Wrong Store
(432) 729-1976
110 W Dallas Street
Marfa, TX 79843
wrongmarfa.com

Prada Marfa
US-90
Valentine, TX 79854

The Chinati Foundation
(432) 729-4362
1 Cavalry Row
Marfa, TX 79843
chinati.org

Galleri Urbane
(432) 386-0590
601 San Antonio Street
Marfa, TX 79843
galleriurbane.com

Ballroom Marfa
(432) 729-3600
108 E San Antonio Street
Marfa, TX 79843
ballroommarfa.org

Eugene Binder Gallery
(432) 729-3900
218 Highland Street
Marfa, TX 79843
eugenebinder.com

Landmarks

Castle Hill
1008 Baylor Street
Austin, TX 78703

Terlingua Cemetery
(432) 371-2234
FM170 & Terlingua
Ghost Town Road
Terlingua, TX 79852

Lodging

Hotel Saint Cecilia
(512) 852-2400
112 Academy Drive
Austin, TX 78704
hotelsaintcecilia.com

Hotel San José
(512) 444-7322
1316 S Congress
Avenue
Austin, TX 78704
sanjosehotel.com

El Cosmico
(432) 729-1950
802 S Highland Avenue
Marfa, TX 79843
elcosmico.com

The Faxonia
Marfa, TX
*airbnb.com/
rooms/13433273*

Tin Valley Retro Rentals
(432) 386-7312
889 Sombrero Peak
Road
Terlingua, TX 79852
*facebook.com/
tinvalleyretrorentals*

Terlingua Ranch Lodge
(432) 371-3146
16000 Terlingua Ranch
Road
Terlingua, TX 79852
terlinguaranch.com

Nightlife/Music

The White Horse
(512) 553-6756
500 Comal Street
Austin, TX 78702
*thewhitehorseaustin.
com*

Emo's
(888) 512-7469
2015 E Riverside Drive
Austin, TX 78741
emosaustin.com

Scoot Inn
(512) 555-5555
1308 E 4th Street
Austin, TX 78702
scootinnaustin.com

Starlight Theatre
(432) 371-2326
631 Ivey Road
Terlingua, TX 79852
thestarlighttheatre.com

Spa/Wellness

Barton Springs Pool
(512) 867-3080
2201 Barton Springs
Road
Austin, TX 78746
*austintexas.gov/
department/
barton-springs-pool*

CHAPTER FIVE: ROUTE 66

Shopping

Rag & Bone Antiques
(806) 373-4637
2816 SW 6th Avenue
Amarillo, TX 79106
rnbantiques.com

Alley Katz Antique
Emporium
(806) 342-5432
2807 SW 6th Avenue
Amarillo, TX 79106
*alleykatzantiques
amarillo.com*

Santa Maria Provisions
(505) 983-2411
125 East Palace Avenue
Sena Plaza Courtyard
Santa Fe, NM 87501
*facebook.com/
santamariaprovisions*

Santa Fe Vintage
Outpost
(505) 603-7403
202 E Palace Avenue
Santa Fe, NM 87501
santafevintage.com

11th Street Records
(702) 527-7990
1023 Fremont Street
Las Vegas, NV 89101
11thstreetrecords.com

Eats

Del Charro
Inn of the Governors
(505) 954-0320
101 W Alameda Street
Santa Fe, NM 87501
delcharro.com

San Marcos Café
(505) 471-9298
3877 NM-14
Santa Fe, NM 87508
*facebook.com/
San-Marcos-
Cafe-163239880399731*

66 Diner
(505) 247-1421
1405 Central Avenue NE
Albuquerque, NM
87106
66diner.com

Grouchy John's Coffee
(702) 778-7553
8520 S Maryland
Parkway
Las Vegas, NV 89123
grouchyjohns.com

Hash House a go go
(702) 804-4646
6800 W Sahara Avenue
Las Vegas, NV 89146
hashhouseagogo.com

Art

Cadillac Ranch
(630) 313-0187
I-40 Frontage Road
Amarillo, TX 79124

Georgia O'Keeffe
Museum
(505) 946-1000
217 Johnson Street
Santa Fe, NM 87501
okeeffemuseum.org

Origami in the Garden
(505) 471-4688
3453 NM-14
Los Cerrillos, NM 87010
*outsidetheboxstudio.
com/oig*

James Turrell's
Akhob exhibit
(702) 730-3150
3720 Las Vegas
Boulevard S, Suite 103
Las Vegas, NV 89158

Landmarks

Palo Duro Canyon
State Park
(806) 488-2227
11450 State Highway
Park Road 5
Canyon, TX 79015
palodurocanyon.com

Cross of the Martyrs
Park
(505) 955-6949
617 Paseo De Peralta
Santa Fe, NM 87501

Madrid Old Coal Town
Museum
(505) 438-3780
2846 Highway 14
Madrid, NM 87010
*facebook.com/madrid
oldcoaltownmuseum*

BioPark Botanic
Garden
(505) 768-2000
2601 Central Ave NW
Albuquerque, NM
87104
*cabq.gov/cultural
services/biopark/
garden*

De Anza Motor Lodge
4301 Central Avenue
NE
Albuquerque, NM
87108
*nps.gov/nr/travel/
route66/de_anza_
motor_lodge_
albuquerque.html*

Neon Museum
(702) 387-6366
770 N Las Vegas
Boulevard
Las Vegas, NV 89101
neonmuseum.org

Lodging

La Fonda on the Plaza
(505) 982-5511
100 E San Francisco
Street
Santa Fe, NM 87501
lafondasantafe.com

Silver Saddle Motel
(505) 395-5563
2810 Cerrillos Road
Santa Fe, NM 87507
*santafesilversaddle
motel.com*

El Rancho Hotel &
Motel
(505) 863-9311
1000 E Hwy 66
Gallup, NM 87301
route66hotels.org

Bright Angel Lodge
& Cabins
(928) 638-2631
Grand Canyon National
Park
9 Village Loop Drive
Grand Canyon Village,
AZ 86023
*grandcanyonlodges.
com/lodging/
bright-angel*

Artisan Hotel Boutique
(702) 214-4000
1501 W Sahara Avenue
Las Vegas, NV 89102
artisanhotel.com

Nightlife/Music

Secreto Lounge
(505) 983-5700
210 Don Gaspar
Avenue
Santa Fe, NM 87501
secretolounge.com

Gold Spike
(702) 476-1082
217 Las Vegas
Boulevard
Las Vegas, NV 89101
goldspike.com

Pinball Hall of Fame
(702) 597-2627
1610 E Tropicana
Avenue
Las Vegas, NV 89119
pinballmuseum.org

Dispensary Lounge
(702) 458-6343
2451 E Tropicana Ave
Las Vegas, NV 89121
thedispensarylounge.
com

Champagne's Cafe
(702) 737-1699
3557 S Maryland
Parkway
Las Vegas, NV 89169
champagnescafe.vegas

El Cortez Hotel
and Casino
(702) 385-5200
600 Fremont Street
Las Vegas, NV 89101
elcortezhotelcasino.com

Atomic Liquors
(702) 982-3000
917 Fremont Street
Las Vegas, NV 89101
atomic.vegas

Don't Tell Mama
(702) 207-0788
517 Fremont Street
Las Vegas, NV 89101
donttellmama.com

Vanguard Lounge
(702) 868-7800
516 Fremont Street
Las Vegas, NV 89101
vanguardlv.com

Spa/Wellness

Santa Rosa Blue Hole
(575) 472-3763
1085 Blue Hole Road
Santa Rosa, NM 88435
santarosabluehole.com

Ten Thousand
Waves Spa
(505) 982-9304
21 Ten Thousand
Waves Way
Santa Fe, NM 87501
tenthousandwaves.com

Phantom Ranch
(303) 297-2757
Grand Canyon National
Park
N Kaibab Trail
North Rim, AZ 86052
grandcanyonlodges.
com/lodging/
phantom-ranch

CHAPTER SIX:
WAY OUT WEST

Shopping

Desert Mountain Herbs
(575) 557-5263
40 Chuparrosa Drive
Rodeo, NM 88056

Chiricahua Gallery
(575) 557-2225
5 Pine Street
Rodeo, NM 88056
chiricahuagallery.org

Finders Keepers
(520) 432-2900
81 Main Street
Bisbee, AZ 85603
fkeepers.com

Culture Pirate
(315) 750-5151
31 Subway Street
Bisbee, AZ 85603
facebook.com/
CulturePirateBisbee

Bisbee Soap & Sundry
(520) 775-2290
74 Main Street
Bisbee, AZ 85603
bisbeesoapandsundry.
com

Óptimo Hatworks
(520) 432-4544
47 Main Street
Bisbee, AZ 85603
optimohatworks.com

Ricochet Vintage Wears
(760) 366-8822
61731 Twentynine
Palms Highway
Joshua Tree, CA 92252
facebook.com/
Ricochet-Vintage-
Wears-323851380017

The End
(760) 418-5536
55872 Twentynine
Palms Highway
Yucca Valley, CA 92284
theendyuccavalley.
tumblr.com

Hoof & the Horn
(760) 365-6100
55840 Twentynine
Palms Highway
Yucca Valley, CA 92284
hoofandthehorn.com

Funky & Darn Near
New
(760) 449-7717
CA-62
Yucca Valley, CA 92284
facebook.com/
funkyandarnnearnew

Trailer Trash
(760) 366-8664
7350 Acoma Trail
Yucca Valley, CA 92284

Eats

Screaming Banshee
Pizza
(520) 432-1300
200 Tombstone
Canyon
Bisbee, AZ 85603
screamingbanshee
pizza.net

AJ's Fine Foods
(480) 314-6500
15031 N Thompson
Peak Parkway
Scottsdale, AZ 85260
ajsfinefoods.com

Art

Central School Project
(520) 432-4866
43 Howell Avenue
Bisbee, AZ 85603
centralschoolproject.
org

Landmarks

White Sands National
Monument
(575) 479-6124
19955 Highway 70
Alamogordo, NM 88310
nps.gov/WHSA

Cholla Cactus Garden
(760) 367-5500
Pinto Basin Road
Joshua Tree National
Park, CA
nps.gov/jotr/planyour
visit/ntrails.htm

Salvation Mountain
Beal Road
Niland, CA 92257
salvationmountain.us

Lodging

Nature Retreat
Las Cruces, NM
airbnb.com/
rooms/10132121

Shady Dell
(520) 432-3567
1 Old Douglas Road
Bisbee, AZ 85603
theshadydell.com

The Dome in the Desert
Joshua Tree, CA 92252
weareinourelement.com/
dome-in-the-desert/

Nightlife/Music

Copper Queen Saloon
Copper Queen Hotel
(520) 432-2216
11 Howell Avenue
Bisbee, AZ 85603
copperqueen.com/
dining-en.html

Pappy & Harriet's
Pioneertown Palace
(760) 365-5956
53688 Pioneertown
Road
Pioneertown, CA 92268
pappyandharriets.com

Joshua Tree Saloon
(760) 366-2250
61835 Twentynine
Palms Highway
Joshua Tree, CA 92252
*thejoshuatreesaloon.
com*

Spa/Wellness

Integratron
(760) 364-3126
2477 Belfield Boulevard
Landers, CA 92285
integratron.com

CHAPTER SEVEN: SOUTHERN SWAMPLANDS

Shopping

shopSCAD
(912) 525-5180
340 Bull Street
Savannah, GA 31402
shopscad.com

ZIA Boutique
(912) 233-3237
325 W Broughton
Street
Savannah, GA 31401
ziaboutique.com

KREWE
(912) 495-5676
216 W Broughton
Street
Savannah, GA 31401
krewe.com

Paris Market &
Brocante
(912) 232-1500
36 W Broughton Street
Savannah, GA 31401
theparismarket.com

The Hidden Hand
Society
2423 DeSoto Avenue
Savannah, Georgia
*thehiddenhand
savannah.com*

Gypsy World
(912) 704-2347
2405 Bull Street
Savannah, GA 31401
*gypsyworldsavannah.
com*

Urban Poppy
(912) 429-3298
2312 Abercorn Street
Savannah, GA 31401
urbanpoppy.com

V & J Duncan Antique
Maps, Prints & Books
(912) 232-0338
12 E Taylor Street
Savannah, GA 31401
vjduncan.com

The Book Lady
Bookstore
(912) 233-3628
6 E Liberty Street
Savannah, GA 31401
*thebookladybookstore.
com*

SecondLine Arts and
Antiques
(504) 875-1924
1209 Decatur Street
New Orleans, LA 70116
*facebook.com/second
lineartsandantiques*

Le Garage Antiques &
Clothing
(504) 522-6639
1234 Decatur Street
New Orleans, LA 70116
*facebook.com/
legarageneworleans*

David's Found Objects
(504) 568-1197
1319 Decatur Street
New Orleans, LA 70116
*davidsfoundobjects.
com*

Sterling Provisions
(917) 309-0259
2402 Royal Street
New Orleans, LA 70117
sterlingprov.com

Euclid Records
(504) 947-4348
3301 Chartres Street
New Orleans, LA 70117
euclidnola.com

Bargain Center
(504) 948-0007
3200 Dauphine Street
New Orleans, LA 70117

The Pop Shop
3212 Dauphine Street
New Orleans, LA 70117

Trashy Diva
(504) 522-4233
537 Royal Street
New Orleans, LA 70130
trashydiva.com

Hemline
(504) 592-0242
609 Chartres Street
New Orleans, LA 70130
shophemline.com

The Revival Outpost
(504) 301-3754
234 Chartres Street
New Orleans, LA 70130
therevivaloutpost.com

United Apparel
Liquidators
(504) 301-4437
518 Chartres Street
New Orleans, LA 70130
shopual.com

Hové Parfumeur
(504) 525-7827
434 Chartres Street
New Orleans, LA 70130
hoveparfumeur.com

Funky Monkey
(504) 899-5587
3127 Magazine Street
New Orleans, LA 70115
funkymonkeynola.com

Lili Vintage Boutique
(504) 891-9311
3329 Magazine Street
New Orleans, LA 70115
lilivintage.com

Eats

Alligator Soul
(912) 232-7899
114 Barnard Street
Savannah, GA 31401
alligatorsoul.com

Circa 1875
(912) 443-1875
48 Whitaker Street
Savannah, GA 31401
circa1875.com

Leopold's Ice Cream
(912) 234-4442
212 E Broughton Street
Savannah, GA 31401
leopoldsicecream.com

Mrs. Wilkes' Dining
Room
(912) 232-5997
107 W Jones Street
Savannah, GA 31401
mrswilkes.com

Cane & Table
(504) 581-1112
1113 Decatur Street
New Orleans, LA 70116
caneandtablenola.com

Cure
(504) 302-2357
4905 Freret Street
New Orleans, LA 70115
curenola.com

Art

Telfair Museums
(912) 790-8800
121 Barnard Street
Savannah, GA 31401
telfair.org

Michalopoulos Gallery
(504) 558-0505
617 Bienville Street
New Orleans, LA 70130
michalopoulos.com

New Orleans Museum
of Art
(504) 658-4100
1 Collins C. Diboll Circle
City Park
New Orleans, LA 70124
noma.org

Landmarks

French Market
(504) 596-3420
1235 N Peters Street
New Orleans, LA 70116
frenchmarket.org

Mercer Williams House
Museum
(912) 236-6352
429 Bull Street
Savannah, GA 31401
mercerhouse.com

Lodging

Catahoula Hotel
(504) 603-2442
914 Union Street
New Orleans, LA 70112
catahoulahotel.com

The Old No. 77 Hotel
& Chandlery
(504) 527-5271
535 Tchoupitoulas
Street
New Orleans, LA 70130
old77hotel.com

Ace Hotel New Orleans
(504) 900-1180
600 Carondelet Street
New Orleans, LA 70130
acehotel.com/
neworleans

The Thunderbird Inn
(912) 232-2661
611 W Oglethorpe
Avenue
Savannah, GA 31401
thethunderbirdinn.com

Nightlife/Music

Vaughan's Lounge
(504) 947-5562
4229 Dauphine Street
New Orleans, LA 70117
facebook.com/
Vaughans-Lounge-
472659709508376

The Apple Barrel Bar
(504) 949-9399
609 Frenchmen Street
New Orleans, LA
facebook.com/
Apple-Barrel-
Bar-117468114938296

The Spotted Cat Music
Club
(504) 943-3887
623 Frenchmen Street
New Orleans, LA 70116
spottedcatmusicclub.
com

Bacchanal Wine
(504) 948-9111
600 Poland Avenue
New Orleans, LA 70117
bacchanalwine.com

Blue Nile
(504) 948-2583
532 Frenchmen Street
New Orleans, LA 70116
bluenilelive.com

d.b.a.
(504) 942-3731
618 Frenchmen Street
New Orleans, LA 70116
dbaneworleans.com

Preservation Hall
(504) 522-2841
726 St Peter Street
New Orleans, LA 70116
preservationhall.com

One Eyed Jacks
(504) 569-8361
615 Toulouse Street
New Orleans, LA 70130
oneeyedjacks.net

Lafitte's Blacksmith
Shop Bar
(504) 593-9761
941 Bourbon Street
New Orleans, LA 70116
lafittesblacksmithshop.
com

CHAPTER EIGHT: ROCK 'N' ROLL HIGHWAY

Shopping

Third Man Records
(615) 891-4393
623 7th Avenue South
Nashville, TN
thirdmanrecords.com/
more/novelties

Cool Stuff Weird Things
(615) 460-1112
4900 Charlotte Pike
Nashville, TN 37209
coolstuffweirdthings.
com

Draper James
(615) 997-3601
2608 12th Avenue South
Nashville, TN 37204
draperjames.com

OPIUMVintage
(337) 837-5358
1629 Shelby Avenue
Nashville, TN 37206
facebook.com/
OPIUMvintage

The Hip Zipper
(615) 228-1942
1008 Forrest Avenue
Nashville, TN 37206
hipzipper.com

Star Struck Vintage
(615) 679-9675
604 Gallatin Avenue,
110
Nashville, TN 37206
starstruckvintage
nashville.com

Local Honey
(615) 915-1354
2009 Belmont Boulevard
Nashville, TN 37212
lhnashville.com

High Class Hillbilly
(615) 840-7328
4604 Gallatin Pike
Nashville, TN 37216
highclasshillbilly.com

Goodbuy Girls
(615) 281-9447
1108 Woodland Street
Nashville, TN 37206
goodbuygirlsnashville.
com

Old Made Good
(615) 432-2882
3701B Gallatin Pike
Nashville, TN 37216
oldmadegoodnashville.
com

Savant Vintage
(615) 385-0856
2302 12th Avenue S
Nashville, TN 37204
savantvintage.com

Two Son
(615) 678-4953
918 Main Street
Nashville, TN 37206
twoson.co

White's Mercantile
(615) 750-5379
2908 12th Avenue
South
Nashville, TN 37204
whitesmercantile.com

Imogene & Willie
(615) 292-5005
2601 12th Avenue
South
Nashville, TN 37204
imogeneandwillie.com

The School of Making
at Alabama Chanin
(256) 760-1090
462 Lane Drive
Florence, AL 35630
alabamachanin.com/
the-school-of-making

Billy Reid
(256) 767-4692
114 N Court Street
Florence, AL 35630
billyreid.com

Atomic Athens
(706) 316-0130
260 W Clayton Street
Athens, GA 30601
facebook.com/
atomicathens

Agora Vintage
(706) 255-2623
233 E Broad Street
Athens, GA 30601
agoravintageshop.com

Wuxtry Records
(706) 369-9428
197 E Clayton Street
Athens, GA 30601
wuxtryrecords.com

Eats

Barista Parlor
(615) 712-9766
519 Gallatin Avenue
Nashville, TN 37206
baristaparlor.com

Five Points Pizza
(615) 915-4174
1012 Woodland Street
Nashville, TN 37206
fivepointspizza.com

Mas Tacos Por Favor
(615) 543-6271
732 Mcferrin Avenue
Nashville, TN 37206
facebook.com/
mastacos

Mickey's Tavern
(615) 852-5228
2907 Gallatin Pike
Nashville, TN 37216
mickeystavern
nashville.com

The Factory
Alabama Chanin
(256) 760-1090
462 Lane Drive
Florence, AL 35630
alabamachanin.com/
the-factory

The National
(706) 549-3450
232 W Hancock Avenue
Athens, GA 30601
thenationalrestaurant.
com

Seabear Oyster Bar
(706) 850-4367
297 Prince Avenue,
Suite 10
Athens, GA 30601
seabearoysterbar.com

Lodging

Urban Cowboy
(347) 840-0525
1603 Woodland Street
Nashville, TN 37206
urbancowboybnb.com/
nashville

Music City Loft
(855) 510-5444
162 4th Avenue N
Nashville, TN 37219
musiccityloft.com

The Graduate Athens
Hotel
(706) 549-7020
295 E Dougherty Street
Athens, GA 30601
graduateathens.com

Nightlife/Music

Ryman Auditorium
(615) 889-3060
116 5th Avenue North
Nashville, TN 37219
ryman.com

Pinewood Social
(615) 751-8111
33 Peabody Street
Nashville, TN 37210
pinewoodsocial.com

The Crying Wolf
(615) 953-6715
823 Woodland Street
Nashville, TN 37206
thecryingwolf.com

The 5 Spot
(615) 650-9333
1006 Forrest Avenue
Nashville, TN 37206
the5spot.club

Grimey's New &
Preloved Music
(615) 254-4801
1604 8th Avenue S
Nashville, TN 37203
grimeys.com

Robert's Western World
(615) 244-9552
416 Broadway B
Nashville, TN 37203
robertswesternworld.
com

Tootsie's Orchid Lounge
(615) 726-0463
422 Broadway
Nashville, TN 37203
tootsies.net

Grand Ole Opry
1 (800) SEE-OPRY
2804 Opryland Drive
Nashville, TN 37214
opry.com

FAME Recording
Studios
(256) 381-0801
603 East Avalon
Avenue
Muscle Shoals, AL
35661
fame2.com

Muscle Shoals Sound
Studios
(256) 978-5151
3614 Jackson Highway
Sheffield, AL 35660
msmusicfoundation.org

Seven Springs Lodge
(256) 370-7218
1292 Mt Mills Road
Tuscumbia, AL 35674
rattlesnakesaloon.net/
lodge.html

Rattlesnake Saloon
(256) 370-7220
1292 Mt Mills Road
Tuscumbia, AL 35674
rattlesnakesaloon.net

The Foundry
The Graduate Athens
Hotel
(706) 549-7020
295 E Dougherty Street
Athens, GA 30601
graduateathens.com/
dining/foundry

40 Watt Club
(706) 549-7871
285 W Washington
Street
Athens, GA 30601
40watt.com

Georgia Theatre
(706) 850-7670
215 N Lumpkin Street
Athens, GA 30601
georgiatheatre.com

Caledonia Lounge
(706) 549-5577
256 W Clayton Street
Athens, GA 30601
caledonialounge.com

CHAPTER NINE: THE GREAT NORTHWEST

Shopping

The Dark Room
(406) 549-1070
109 W Main Street
Missoula, MT 59802
darkroomofmontana.
com

Carlo's One Night Stand
(406) 543-6350
109 S 3rd Street W
Missoula, MT 59801
carlosonenightstand.
com

Betty's Divine
(406) 721-4777
509 S Higgins Avenue
Missoula, MT 59801
bettysdivine.com

Rockin' Rudy's
(406) 542-0077
237 Blaine Street
Missoula, MT 59801
rockinrudys.com

Crystal Winters
(406) 862-6104
232 Central Avenue
Whitefish, MT 59937
crystalwinters.com

S. M. Bradford
(406) 862-6333
206 Central Avenue
Whitefish, MT 59937
*facebook.com/
smbradfordco*

Trove Vintage
Boutique
(206) 297-6068
2204 NW Market Street
Seattle, WA 98107
*trovevintage.blogspot.
com*

Lucky Vintage
(206) 789-8191
5424 Ballard Avenue NW
Seattle, WA 98107
luckyvintageseattle.com

Sonic Boom Records
(206) 297-2666
2209 NW Market Street
Seattle, WA 98107
sonicboomrecords.com

Juniper
(206) 838-7496
3314 E Spring Street
Seattle, WA 98122
juniperinmadrona.com

Les Amis
(206) 632-2877
3420 Evanston
Avenue N
Seattle, WA 98103
lesamis-inc.com

Show Pony
(206) 706-4188
702 N 35th Street
Seattle, WA 98103
showponyboutique.com

Fremont Sunday
Market
(206) 781-6776
3401 Evanston
Avenue N
Seattle, WA 98103
fremontmarket.com

Pike Place Market
(206) 682-7453
85 Pike Street
Seattle, WA 98101
pikeplacemarket.org

Hands of the World
Pike Place Market
(206) 622-1696
1501 Pike Place #428
Seattle, WA 98101
handsoftheworld.com

Conscious Wear
Pike Place Market
(206) 682-1629
1501 Pike Place
Seattle, WA 98101
*facebook.com/pages/
Conscious-Wear/
609999369070187*

Earth Wind and Fire
Boutique
Pike Place Market
(206) 448-2529
1514 Pike Place #13
Seattle, WA 98101
*earthwindandfire
boutique.com*

2nd Hand GALA
Pike Place Market
(206) 623-3716
1501 Pike Place #324
Seattle, WA 98101
*facebook.com/
2ndHandGALA*

Eats

Zootown Brew
(406) 543-2549
121 W Broadway Street
Missoula, MT 59802
zootownbrew.com

Catalyst Cafe &
Espresso Bar
Red Bird
(406) 542-1337
111 N Higgins Avenue
Missoula, MT 59802
thecatalystcafe.com

Break Espresso
(406) 728-7300
432 N Higgins Avenue
Missoula, MT 59802
*facebook.com/Break
EspressoMissoula*

Butterfly Herbs
(406) 728-8780
232 N Higgins Avenue
Missoula, MT 59802
butterflyherbs.com

Portage Bay Cafe
(206) 462-6400
391 Terry Avenue N
Seattle, WA 98109
portagebaycafe.com

Lockspot Cafe
(206) 789-4865
3005 NW 54th Street
Seattle, WA 98107
thelockspotcafe.com

Art

Miracle of America
Museum
(406) 883-6804
36094 Memory Lane
Polson, MT 59860
*miracleofamerica
museum.org*

Museum of Pop Culture
(206) 770-2700
325 5th Avenue N
Seattle, WA 98109
mopop.org

Landmarks

Glacier National Park
(406) 888-7800
64 Grinnell Drive
West Glacier, MT 59936
nps.gov/glac

Olympic National Park
(360) 565-3130
3002 Mt Angeles Road
Port Angeles, WA
98362
nps.gov/olym/

Mount Rainier National
Park
(360) 569-2211
39000 State Route
706 E
Ashford, WA 98304
nps.gov/mora

Aurora Bridge
Aurora Avenue N
Seattle, WA 98103

Ballard Locks
(206) 783-7059
3015 NW 54th Street
Seattle, WA 98107
ballardlocks.org

Seattle Metaphysical
Library
(206) 329-1794
2220 NW Market Street
Seattle, WA 98107
*seattlemetaphysical
library.org*

Lodging

Shady Spruce Hostel
(406) 285-1197
204 E Spruce Street
Missoula, MT 59802
shadysprucehostel.com

Gaynor Ranch Bed and
Breakfast
(406) 883-3807
32318 Bisson Lane
Polson, MT 59860
gaynorranch.net

Bridge Street Cottage
(406) 837-2785
309 Bridge Street
Bigfork, MT 59911
*bridgestreetcottages.
com*

Whitefish Hostel
(406) 863-9450
28 Lupfer Avenue
Whitefish, MT 59937
whitefishhostel.com

Hotel Ballard
(206) 789-5012
5216 Ballard Avenue
NW
Seattle, WA 98107
*hotelballardseattle.
com/en-us*

The Ace Hotel
(206) 448-4721
2423 1st Avenue
Seattle, WA 98121
acehotel.com/seattle

Nightlife/Music

The Wilma
(406) 728-9865
131 Higgins Avenue
Missoula, MT 59802
thewilma.com

Top Hat Lounge
(406) 728-9865
134 W Front Street
Missoula, MT 59802
tophatlounge.com

King's Hardware
(206) 782-0027
5225 Ballard Avenue
NW
Seattle, WA 98107
kingsballard.com

Chop Suey
(206) 538-0556
1325 E Madison Street
Seattle, WA 98122
chopsuey.com

Neumos Crystal Ball
Reading Room
(206) 709-9442
925 E Pike Street
Seattle, WA 98122
neumos.com

The Crocodile
(206) 441-4618
2200 2nd Avenue
Seattle, WA 98121
thecrocodile.com

Landmarks

Brennan's Wave
Clark Fork River
Missoula, MT 59802

Zoo Town Surfers
(406) 546-0370
5077 Old US Hwy 10 W
Alberton, MT 59820
zootownsurfers.com

Spa/Wellness

Apothecary Esthetics
(406) 540-2766
200 E Pine Street
Missoula, MT 59802
*apothecaryesthetics.
com*

Breweries

Imagine Nation
Brewing Co.
(406) 926-1251
1151 W Broadway Street
Missoula, MT 59802
*imaginenationbrewing.
com*

Great Burn Brewing
(406) 317-1557
2230 McDonald
Avenue
Missoula, MT 59801
greatburnbrewing.com

Flathead Lake
Brewing Co.
(406) 542-3847
424 N Higgins Avenue
Missoula, MT 59802
*flatheadlakebrewing.
com*

PHOTO CREDITS

Allister Ann 8, 9, 11
(L), 16, 17, 20 (R), 21
(foreground), 27 (R),
28–37, 39–48 (R), 50,
56, 57 (background),
63, 67 (middle), 109, 111
(L), 127 (foreground),
128(R), 129–143, 149,
151, 155, 165 (R), 168
(R), 171, 172, 200
(bottom), 205, 213, 214,
220–221 (background),
222, 224 (top), 227–234,
235 (R), 237 (L)

Ben Alleman 1, 11 (R),
19, 21 (background), 65
(top), 67 (bottom), 100-
101, 102 (bottom), 104
(top), 118 (bottom), 120,
126–127 (background),
128 (L), 144, 145, 154
(top), 159 (top), 160,
161, 162-163, 165 (L),
197 (foreground), 198,
201–203, 208, 237 (top)

c/o Krystal Bick 13, 24
(L), 121, 154 (bottom),
159 (bottom), 167 (R),
225, 235 (L), 237 (R),
238

Amanda Bjorn & David
Donaldson 2, 51, 53, 55

c/o Christine Cameron
110, 111 (R), 241 (top)

c/o Kristin Diable 200
(top), 207, 219

Andi Eaton 25, 48 (R),
54, 67 (top), 81, 83,
84 (top), 86, 91, 92, 95
(middle), 96, 98 (top),
99, 123, 124, 164, 189
(top), 190, 192, 208
(bottom), 216–218, all
Polaroids throughout

Keiko Lynn Groves 5,
20 (L), 22, 60 (L), 71,
80 (background), 82,
84 (bottom), 85, 87–90,
93, 95 (top & bottom),
97, 98 (bottom), 147 (L),
150–151 (background),
152, 153, 156, 157,
166, 168 (L), 173, 196
(background)

Hunter Holder 6, 15, 27
(L), 38, 57 (foreground),
58–62, 65 (bottom),
66, 68–69, 73, 75,
77, 174–178, 180, 183
(bottom), 185, 186, 189
(bottom), 191, 193

Charlotte Fassler &
Aza Ziegler 18, 24 (R),
102 (top), 103, 104
(bottom), 105, 106, 107,
112, 113, 115, 117, 118
(top), 125

Krystal Frame 146, 147,
201, 215

Kendra Jones 224
(bottom), 239, 241
(bottom)

c/o Michelle Lester 23

Marianna Massey 199

c/o Sonora Mindling-
Werling 221, 223, 226,
243

Akasha Rabut 179

c/o Rebecca Rebouche
181, 183 (top), 195

c/o Kaylyn Weir by
Hello Miss Lovely 14,
74, 79